PEOPLES
of
AFRICA

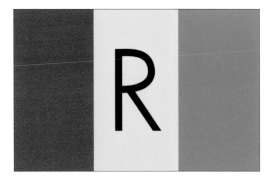

Rwanda

Saint Helena

São Tomé and Príncipe

Senegal

Seychelles

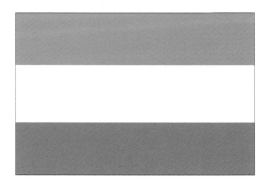

Sierra Leone

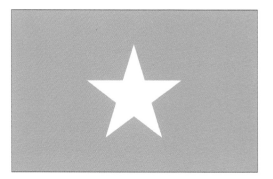

Somalia

PEOPLES
of
AFRICA

Volume 8
Réunion–Somalia

MARSHALL CAVENDISH
NEW YORK • LONDON • TORONTO • SYDNEY

Marshall Cavendish Corporation
99 White Plains Road
Tarrytown, New York 10591-9001

Reference Edition 2003

Consultants:
Bryan Callahan, Department of History, Johns Hopkins University
Kevin Shillington

Pronunciation Consultant: Nancy Gratton

Contributing authors:
   Fiona Macdonald
   Elizabeth Paren
   Kevin Shillington
   Gillian Stacey
   Philip Steele

Discovery Books
   Managing Editor: Paul Humphrey
   Project Editor: Helen Dwyer
   Text Editor: Valerie J. Weber
   Design Concept: Ian Winton
   Designer: Barry Dwyer
   Cartographer: Stefan Chabluk

Marshall Cavendish
   Editorial Director: Paul Bernabeo
   Editor: Marian Armstrong

The publishers would like to thank the following for their permission to reproduce photographs:
   Corbis (Hulton-Deutsch Collection: 449); Robert Estall Photo Library (Carol Beckwith/Angela Fisher: 463); Mary Evans Picture Library (432); gettyone Stone (Manfred Mehlig: 444; Colin Prior: 447); Robert Harding Picture Library (Explorer: 436, 440; Jennifer Fry: 439); Hutchison Library (421; Juliet Highet: 446; Crispin Hughes: 460; Liz McLeod: 453, 455 top; Trevor Page: 417, 420; Bernard Régent: 435 top); Panos Pictures (Martin Adler: 425; Jeremy Hartley: 430, 435 bottom, 441, 443 top, 455 bottom, 461; Fred Hoogervorst: 438; Caroline Penn: 457 top; Giacomo Pirozzi: cover, 427 top, 427 bottom, 428, 429; Betty Press: 414; Clive Shirley: 456; Jon Spaull: 451, 452, 457 bottom; Liba Taylor: 418; Hamish Wilson: 458, 462; Gisèle Wulfsohn: 437); Alexander Schulenburg (423); Spectrum (413); Still Pictures (Adrian Arbib: 419; John Isaac: 442); Topham Picturepoint (411); Tropix Photographic Library (Eric Roberts: 412); Redferns Music Picture Library (Tim Hall: 443 bottom)

(cover) Comorian women sing and dance, beating the time with wooden sticks.

Editor's note: Many systems of dating have been used by different cultures throughout history. *Peoples of Africa* uses B.C.E. (Before Common Era) and C.E. (Common Era) instead of B.C. (Before Christ) and A.D. (Anno Domini, "In the Year of the Lord") out of respect for the diversity of the world's peoples.

Library of Congress Cataloging-in-Publication Data

Peoples of Africa.
      p. cm.
   Includes bibliographical references and index.
   Contents: v. 1. Algeria–Botswana — v. 2. Burkina–Faso-Comoros — v. 3. Congo, Democratic Republic of–Eritrea — v. 4. Ethiopia–Guinea — v. 5. Guinea-Bissau–Libya — v. 6. Madagascar–Mayotte — v. 7. Morocco–Nigeria — v. 8. Réunion–Somalia — v. 9. South Africa–Tanzania — v. 10. Togo–Zimbabwe — v. 11. Index.
   ISBN 0-7614-7158-8 (set)
      1. Ethnology—Africa—Juvenile literature. 2. Africa—History—Juvenile literature. 3. Africa—Social life and customs—Juvenile literature. I. Marshall Cavendish Corporation.

GN645 .P33 2000
305.8'0096—dc21

                                                    99-088550

      ISBN 0-7614-7158-8 (set)
      ISBN 0-7614-7166-9 (vol. 8)

Printed in Hong Kong

06   05   04   03   6   5   4   3   2

Contents

RÉUNION

RÉUNION IS AN OVERSEAS REGION OF FRANCE, lying in the Indian Ocean.

Jagged volcanic peaks run across Réunion diagonally. The volcanic crater of Piton de la Fournaise is still active, last erupting in 1998. The mountains divide the island into two parts: the east is green and moist, while the south and west lie in the shelter of the mountains and so remain dry.

French, Africans, and Asians

Réunion (rae-YOON-yohn), Africa's remote outpost in the Indian Ocean, does not appear in historical records until four to five hundred years ago, when Portuguese, Dutch, and English seafarers began to anchor there.

The French East India Company, which needed a refueling stop on the route to India, claimed and took possession of the island in 1638 C.E. Settlers arrived from France and slaves were brought from Madagascar and the African mainland. French farmers grew coffee and spices and supplied farm produce to the larger French colony of Mauritius. Loggers cleared forests, and unique bird species were hunted to extinction.

In the 1790s the Réunion slaves demanded freedom and equality. Some escaped and hid out in wild mountainous country. During the early 1800s, the British

---

CLIMATE

Most of Réunion has a warm, tropical climate, though it is cooler in the highlands. Southeasterly winds bring heavy rains to the island's east side between April and October. Réunion lies in the path of severe storms called cyclones.

Average January temperature: *80°F (27°C)*

Average July temperature: *70°F (21°C)*

Average annual precipitation: *56 in. (142 cm)*

---

attacked and occupied the islands. They planted sugarcane, which became the chief crop after French rule returned in 1815. The slave trade was banned in 1817, and in 1848 all remaining slaves, numbering about sixty thousand, were released. Workers brought in from India, China, and Southeast Asia replaced slave labor, though their working conditions were notoriously poor.

Power remained in the hands of the wealthy French plantation owners on the coast. Small-time French farmers had to make a living on the mountain plateaus of the interior. The majority of the population rapidly blended by marriage to become Métis—people of mixed black African, Asian, and European descent.

Réunion's economy had trouble competing on the world sugar market, and political unrest grew. A left-wing political movement named the Committee for Democratic and Social Action was established in 1936. It called for an end to the island's colonial

Many old French colonial buildings may be seen on the Avenue de la Victoire in the capital, Saint-Denis. Saint-Denis lies on the north coast of the island.

status and for union with France. However, the French elite believed they would profit the most by keeping the island as a colony.

Réunion became an overseas department of France in 1946. The island's status was upgraded in 1974, when it became a full administrative region of France.

The chief political demand since then has been for economic improvement and for moving administrative and ruling power from Paris to Réunion's general and regional councils. The division of wealth along ethnic lines, with those of black African descent suffering the most poverty, has caused increasing resentment.

Réunion Today

Economically and politically, Réunion remains closely tied to France. Unemployment is high, and many basic

FACTS AND FIGURES

Status: *Overseas region of France*

Capital: *Saint-Denis*

Other towns: *Saint-Pierre, Saint-Louis*

Area: *969 square miles (2,510 square kilometers)*

Population: *700,000*

Population density: *722 per square mile (279 per square kilometer)*

Peoples: *64 percent Métis (mixed African-Asian-European descent); 28 percent South and Southeast Asian descent; 2 percent Chinese descent; 2 percent European (mostly French) descent; 1 percent eastern African descent; 3 percent other*

Official language: *French*

Currency: *French franc*

National day: *Bastille Day (July 14)*

Country's name: *Réunion means "a gathering" in French. The name was chosen in 1793, during the French Revolution.*

Time line:	French East India Company claims island	Slaves imported	Slave trade abolished	Labor begins to be imported from India	Réunion becomes an overseas department of France	Becomes full administrative region of France
	1638 C.E.	1664	1817	1860	1946	1974

411

items must be imported, including fuel, household goods, metals, and many foods.

Sugar supplies three-quarters of the island's income, and the same industry provides molasses (raw sugar syrup) and rum. Other crops include corn, potatoes, eggplant, tropical fruits such as guavas, pineapples, and bananas, and spinachlike vegetables called *brèdes* (BREHDZ). Coastal waters produce fine lobsters. Fragrant geraniums and vanilla pods are grown for use in the perfume industry. Cement is manufactured and stone is quarried. Tourism is growing rapidly. There are ports for large ships, and there is an international airport. A French military base with a garrison of four thousand people plays a substantial part in Réunion's economy; maintaining the base and garrison creates many jobs for the people of Réunion, while the soldiers spend their wages locally.

Fertile land is in short supply. Farmland takes up about one-fifth of the island, with large sugarcane plantations accounting for most of it. Since the mountainous interior forces most people to live along the coast, the coastal areas are densely populated. Many people have immigrated to Madagascar or France.

Old colonial buildings and plantation homes, with their verandas and intricate ironwork, may still be seen. General housing varies from modern city dwellings, built in concrete, to rural shacks.

Islanders enjoy good health care, with one doctor for every 605 residents. Women can expect to live to seventy-seven years and men to seventy-one years old. Many older people have had no formal schooling, but today education modeled on the French system is compulsory, with elementary schools, high schools, and the French Indian Ocean University in Saint-Denis (seh-duh-NEE).

Language and People

French is the island's official language, and it is the language used in schools. Almost one-third of the population speaks standard French, including those who speak it as a second language. Most islanders speak Réunion Creole, a local dialect of French that has become a language in itself. The most common Asian language still heard is Tamil, originally from southern India.

Almost nine out of every ten islanders are Roman Catholic, and Catholic shrines are found by roadsides, in caves, and on cliff tops. The rest of the population is primarily Muslim, but there are a number of Hindus as well. Most large towns have both a mosque and a Hindu temple. Southern Indian Hindu festivals such as Pandialé (pahn-dee-AHL-ae), or Tamadee, and Cavadee still take place. During these celebrations, devout Hindus show their

High and dry: a fisherman hangs out his catch by the highway. Fish and shellfish, often served with rice, are an important source of food on Réunion.

A young woman of Indian descent puts on her finery to attend one of Réunion's Hindu festivals. Many Asians came to the island to work as contract laborers in the 1800s.

powers of endurance by walking on glowing embers and piercing their flesh with silver needles.

The harvest of some of Réunion's chief crops provides a reason for local festivals and celebrations. Three of the biggest, lasting for a week to ten days, are the Vanilla Festival in Bras-Panon in May, the Saffron Festival in Saint-Joseph in August, and the Litchi Festival in Saint-Denis in December.

French food is popular and available in many restaurants. Ginger, saffron, and coconut flavor food in Réunion. African (or "Creole") cooking uses dried fish, rice, chili peppers, hot sauces, a spicy tomato and

vegetable chutney called *rougail* (roo-GEHL), and *graines* (GRAHNZ), which are white beans, lentils, and peas. Local seafood is popular, and mountain rivers provide trout and eels. Indian contributions to cuisine include curries, *samosas* (sah-MOE-zahz), which are triangular pastry parcels of meat or vegetables, and very sweet candies.

Réunion has a lively musical life, with folk and pop styles similar to the *sega* (SAE-gah) popular on Mauritius (see MAURITIUS). The sega dance of Réunion has been influenced by French dances such as the quadrille and by the *maloya* (muh-LOE-yah), a slave dance with a slow rhythm similar to the blues. The bands that accompany the dancing play on Western instruments, such as accordions, as well as local ones, such as the *houleur* (OO-LUHR), which is a hide-covered drum, and the *caiambe* (kie-YAHM-bae), which is similar to the maraca.

Let's Talk Kréol Rényoné

Réunion Creole, or Kréol Rényoné *(KREE-oel rehn-YOEN-ae), is spoken by 91 percent of islanders, whether of African, Asian, or European descent. There are two chief dialects. The town version is nearest to standard French, while the rural version includes more words belonging to the Bantu language group of the African mainland.*

salam	*hello*
(sal-AHM)	
mérsi	*thank you*
(MARE-see)	
vil	*town*
(VEEL)	
bwa	*forest*
(BWAH)	
volay	*chicken, poultry*
(voe-LAY)	

RWANDA

RWANDA IS A SMALL LANDLOCKED COUNTRY of mountains and lakes.

Most of Rwanda lies at over 5,000 feet (1,500 meters) above sea level. The Virunga Mountains of the northwest rise to 14,787 feet (4,500 meters) at Karisimbi Volcano. In the far west is Lake Kivu and its outflow, the Rusizi River. Plateaus in the center of the country descend to the Tanzanian border, a low-lying region dotted with lakes.

CLIMATE

Rwanda's high altitude keeps it cool. Wet seasons last from October to December, as well as from March through May.

Average January temperature: *67°F (19°C)*
Average July temperature: *70°F (21°C)*
Average annual precipitation: *40 in. (102 cm)*

A Land Divided

Historians writing about Rwanda (ruh-WAHN-duh) and its southern neighbor, Burundi, tend to agree on just one fact—that the Twa (TWAH) people have lived there longer than anyone else. The Twa are part of a family of central African peoples of short height and slight build. For thousands of years they hunted wild animals and gathered food such as fruits and honey in the forests.

A group of Twa hunter-gatherers from the southwest performs a dance. The short, petite-framed Twa were probably the first Rwandans, but today they make up only a small portion of the population.

414

Probably over one thousand years ago, a people called the Hutu (HOO-too) moved onto the Twa land. They were part of a greater movement of iron-using peoples, speakers of Bantu languages, who migrated out of western central Africa over many centuries (see CAMEROON). The Hutu were farmers, who began to clear the forests for growing crops.

By about seven hundred years ago, another Bantu people had entered the region—the Tutsi (TOOT-see), herders of long-horned cattle. The origins of the Tutsi are lost in history, but the fact remains that the Tutsi began to dominate the Hutu farmers, even though they were greatly outnumbered by them. The difference between the groups was based less on major ethnic differences than on economics and social class. The Tutsi derived their economic and social power from their wealth in cattle. The Hutu farmers were forced to work for the Tutsi herders, who controlled all use of land. Arrangements regarding farming, grazing, military service, and tribute, or taxation, were governed by binding social contracts between individual Hutu and a series of Tutsi overlords, who were responsible to the king. The territory was already crowded, and the division of the land was neither practical nor just.

The Tutsi founded a kingdom near Kigali (kee-GAH-lee) in the 1400s C.E. The Tutsi kingdom extended its control throughout central Rwanda during the 1600s. Two hundred years later Rwanda reached the height of its power as a united state. Its warriors were recruited only from the Tutsi, with the Hutu serving as porters or

FACTS AND FIGURES

Official name: *Republika y'u Rwanda*

Status: *Independent state*

Capital: *Kigali*

Major towns: *Butare, Ruhengeri, Gisenyi*

Area: *10,169 square miles (26,338 square kilometers)*

Population: *8,200,000*

Population density: *806 per square mile (311 per square kilometer)*

Peoples: *85 percent Hutu; 14 percent Tutsi; 1 percent Twa*

Official languages: *Kinyarwanda and French*

Currency: *Rwanda franc*

National day: *National Day (July 1)*

Country's name: Rwanda *means "northern land" in the Kinyarwanda language.*

servants. Young Tutsi males were sent to the royal court to be trained in weapons and warfare as well as in proper manners, in dancing, and poetry. The *mwami* (MWAH-mee), or king, had absolute power over his subjects; indeed, he was believed to be descended from the gods.

Europeans Promote Ethnic Division

Before long, Europeans entered this region, searching for the source of the Nile River. The Germans came to control the region in 1890 as part of the great "scramble for Africa," when European powers competed to seize vast areas of Africa for themselves.

Time line:	Hutu settle land of the Twa	Tutsi dominate Hutu majority	Tutsi found kingdom near Kigali	Rwanda comes under German control	Belgium takes control during World War I
	ca. 900s C.E.	1300s	1400s	1890	1916

By 1914 the same European powers were at war with each other. In 1916 the Germans were ousted from Rwanda, and Belgium took control. Belgian rule continued after the end of World War I in 1918, and in 1923 the League of Nations (the forerunner of the United Nations) appointed Belgium to continue as the colonial power in Rwanda and neighboring Burundi (see BURUNDI). The territory was called Ruanda-Urundi.

The Germans and the Belgians ruled the territory in a similar way, allowing the Tutsi minority to keep their traditional privileges. It was the Tutsi who gained jobs in the European administration or the army, and who were educated by Christian missionaries. The Hutu majority, now further down the social scale than ever, were treated as peasants. Identity documents defined families as Tutsi or Hutu and entitled them to either privileges or oppression. This was an easy way for the new rulers to keep the greater part of the population tied to the land and unable to cause political trouble.

Unfortunately, by making official the distinction between the two groups, the colonial rulers created a problem for the future. Rwandan society had been much more fluid and changeable in precolonial times, with little social conflict. There had always been a high degree of intermarriage between Tutsi and Hutu. People with high status and wealth became Tutsi, while the rest were Hutu.

For the next thirty years, pressure began to build up among the Hutu, fueled by a sense of injustice. By 1952 the Hutu were demanding a complete reform of Rwandan society. In 1959 the mwami died under mysterious circumstances. An extreme Tutsi faction attempted to kill all Hutu political leaders, and this brought about a bloody revenge by the Hutu, which the Belgians did little or nothing to stop.

Conflicts within the Country

In 1961 Rwandans voted to become an independent republic, and in 1962 Grégoire Kayibanda, a Hutu, became president. Some Tutsi fled into Burundi, and in 1963 they launched cross-border raids, killing twenty thousand. Ten years later another Hutu faction forced Kayibanda from power. General Juvénal Habyarimana led the new government. In 1981 he made Rwanda into a one-party, socialist state. The following years saw massacres in Burundi (see BURUNDI) and Hutu refugees pouring into Rwanda. There were severe droughts and storms and a fall in world prices of coffee, a major crop. Times were very hard.

A Decade of Genocide

In 1990 a group of Tutsi exiles based in Uganda, the Rwanda Patriotic Front (RPF), launched a cross-border war against the government. A peace deal was signed in 1993, but in the following year Habyarimana and also the Burundian head of state (both Hutu) were killed in an airplane crash, probably after their aircraft encountered hostile fire.

Hutu militias, who had opposed the peace deal negotiated by Habyarimana,

League of Nations appoints Belgium to rule indirectly through Tutsi leaders	Start of the independence movement	Tutsi-Hutu conflict; 100,000 Tutsi killed	Independence; Hutu Grégoire Kayibanda becomes president; Tutsi flee country
1923	**1952**	**1959**	**1962**

A refugee family at a food distribution point in northern Rwanda. They are just a few of the countless people displaced from their homes by the fighting of the 1990s.

decided to establish a purely Hutu state. The individual people of Rwanda were forced to choose whether they were Hutu or Tutsi, even though many families were mixed. The Hutu militias murdered moderate Hutu politicians and others who believed in creating a democratic government that was not based on ethnic division. They went on to attack all Tutsi. In just three months Hutu militias massacred between 500,000 and 800,000 people, most of them Tutsi.

The RPF responded by attacking the capital, Kigali, and capturing it in July 1994. The French, who had supported the former Hutu regime, moved troops into the southern half of Rwanda. Guarded by the French troops, the Hutu militias organized a massive exodus from Rwanda. Two million Hutu, including many who had taken part in the genocide, crossed into Zaire (today called the Democratic Republic of Congo).

The troubles of Rwanda proved to be a disaster for this region of Africa as a whole. In 1995 the RPF-dominated Rwandan government backed Tutsi who had killed Hutu living in Zaire, and so Zaire nearly went to war with Rwanda. The crisis was averted when many Hutu living in Zaire were allowed back into Rwanda.

Exiled Tutsi raid from Burundi; 20,000 killed	Hutu General Juvénal Habyarimana forces Kayibanda out	One-party socialist state declared	Massacres in Burundi cause flood of Hutu refugees
1963	**1973**	**1981**	**1980s**

The Hutu militia remained an active force in the refugee camps of eastern Zaire, rearming and attacking local Tutsi. When local Zairean Tutsi reacted to these attacks, a large-scale, antigovernment rebellion erupted in eastern Zaire. The RPF government in Rwanda seized the opportunity to settle old scores. The Rwandan army crossed the border, joined the rebels, and attacked the Hutu militia in the Zairean refugee camps. Most of the militia fled into the forest, leaving the bulk of the Hutu civilian refugees free to trek back into Rwanda, away from the fighting of the Zairean civil war.

The Rwandan military went on to play a leading part in the successful rebellion that toppled the government of President Mobutu Sese Seko in Zaire, and that country was renamed the Democratic Republic of Congo in 1997 (see CONGO, DEMOCRATIC REPUBLIC OF). Peace, however, did not return to the region. Hutu militias remained in eastern Democratic Republic of Congo and continued to threaten the security of Rwanda. The Rwandan government thus fell out with their former allies, the new government of the Democratic Republic of Congo, and the Rwandan army became heavily involved in a continuing civil war in the region.

In Rwanda itself the consequences of the genocide lived on. Widespread distrust between surviving Tutsi and the Hutu who had returned from the Democratic Republic of Congo remained. Small-scale atrocities were committed by both sides as cross-border raids by Hutu militia continued and the mainly Tutsi army responded with reprisals.

An international court of justice was set up in Tanzania to try the leaders of the genocide, but no more than a handful were arrested or brought to trial. Inside Rwanda the government arrested many thousands of people suspected of genocide and held

them in overcrowded prisons. Some have been tried, convicted, and executed, but the process is slow, the government lacks resources, and thousands remain in appalling prison conditions. It is clear that the bitterness, suffering, and conflict provoked by the terrible genocide will continue to dominate the region for many years to come.

This boldly patterned basketry is the work of Rwandan women living in exile in the refugee camps of Tanzania. The Rwandan conflict has affected all the surrounding countries.

1990	1993	1994	1995	2000
Rwanda Patriotic Front (RPF) attacks government	Peace deal	Civil war; Hutu massacre more than 500,000; Tutsi RPF takes control; 2 million Hutu refugees flee to Zaire	War crimes tribunal	Many thousands still await trial in Rwandan prisons

A Rwandan farmer picks coffee beans from his bushes. Coffee is widely grown as a cash crop in Rwanda, and it is the only important export in times of peace.

A Crowded Country

Rwanda is Africa's most densely populated nation. About 95 percent of Rwandans live in the countryside. People live in scattered settlements in family groups. Older homes are made of sun-dried mud bricks and roofed with thatch. Concrete and grooved iron are also common building materials.

About 40 percent of the land is suitable for farming, with the richest soils in the northwest and the river valleys. Nine out of ten Rwandan workers are farmers, most able to grow just enough food to support themselves or to supply the local market. They produce sweet potatoes, corn, bananas, plantains, cassava, sorghum, and millet. Cash crops, grown for export on larger farms, include coffee (the most important crop), tea, sugarcane, and pyrethrum, a plant used to make insecticides. Some 20 percent of land is used as pasture by sheep, goats, and cattle. Lakes Kivu, Muhazi, and Mugesera provide fish.

About 20 percent of the land is still forested, but people have stripped most of the original natural cover. No longer anchored by roots, soil has been washed away by tropical rains, causing erosion.

Rwanda is not rich in natural resources, although it has minerals such as cassiterite (from which tin is obtained) and wolframite (from which tungsten is obtained). Methane gas from Lake Kivu fuels trucks and is used to manufacture fertilizers. There is hydroelectric power, but energy also has to be imported from the Democratic Republic of Congo, and only one home in five has electricity. Industries include textiles, cement, soap, processed foods, and furniture manufacture.

Devastated by years of civil war and strife, the Rwandan economy has also suffered because of the country's distance from major seaports. Roads are poor and railroads are nonexistent.

Daily Life in Rwanda

Life expectancy is only forty-one years for men and forty-two years for women. The country faces many severe medical problems, including kwashiorkor, a disease caused by a poor diet. AIDS is widespread.

The education system is based both on state schools and religious missions, with about 70 percent of men and 52 percent of women able to read and write. As is often traditional in Africa, many families do not believe in educating girls, so girls are often kept at home and out of school. Schooling is compulsory from the ages of seven to fifteen, but in practice many children never attend school, especially during times of conflict. There is a national university, with colleges in Butare (boo-TAH-rae) and Ruhengeri (roo-en-GEH-ree).

The Belgians brought Roman Catholic Christianity to the region. It is still followed by about 56 percent of the population. Some 12 percent are Protestant Christian and about 9 percent are Muslim. The remainder follow African religions. They believe that the natural world is the domain of spirits and gods, that sorcery

In northwestern Rwanda, women wear brightly colored wraps and head scarves. They spread out their goods for market—cornmeal, plantains, tomatoes, and vegetables.

> ## Eating for Status
>
> *In most societies throughout history, the wealthy or noble classes have taken pride in feasting more lavishly than the poor peasants. However, the Tutsi warriors always took pride in eating less than the Hutu. During the day, the Tutsi ate just two meals of curdled milk (similar to yogurt). In the evening they ate a simple meal of milk, beans or plantains, and salty butter. The Hutu farmers, however, ate two large, starchy meals each day. The two groups even drank different beverages. The Tutsi enjoyed banana beer or mead (an alcoholic drink made from honey), while the Hutu drank millet beer.*

can heal or harm people, and that the spirits of one's ancestors live on.

Many Rwandans wear Western dress—shirts or T-shirts, pants or shorts, cotton

dresses—sometimes covered by cloaks or blankets. Many women still wear a cotton wrap called a *pagne* (PAHN-yuh) with a blouse and a shawl. Traditional costume, as worn by Tutsi dancers, includes beaded collars and headdresses resembling a lion's mane.

A typical Rwandan meal is made up of sweet potatoes or of cornmeal boiled into a stiff porridge. This is served with peas or beans and sometimes chicken or fish.

Peoples and Languages

Although the violence between Hutu and Tutsi remains extreme, their ways of life are no longer different. Many families include people of both Hutu and Tutsi descent, and for them the recent violence has been especially tragic and painful. The Twa still survive by hunting in their ancestral lands but make up less than one percent of the population. They suffered severely in the civil war and massacres and have also been affected by the clearance of the forests where they live.

All Rwandans are together known as Banyarwanda (bahn-yar-WAHN-dah: the people of Rwanda), and 98 percent of them use Kinyarwanda (KEEN-yar-WAHN-dah), a language of the Bantu family. The Twa speak a dialect of the language. French, the chief language of the Belgian colonialists, is still used for all official and government business but is of limited everyday use. The eastern African coastal language, Swahili (swah-HEE-lee), reached Rwanda through merchants and traders and is widely understood in towns.

Drums and Praise

The Tutsi danced in order to honor the mwami and other overlords, writing poems and singing songs in praise of their bravery, nobility, and wealth in cattle. The Hutu dances, which varied from one region to another, centered more upon farming life through the year. The dances are still performed. Musical instruments were made of wood, horn, and hide and included xylophones. Drums were the special preserve of the Tutsi royal court.

With stylized gestures, a group of Tutsi dancers performs on a dance floor of beaten earth. They wear headbands topped with flowing "manes."

SAINT HELENA

THE LONELY ISLAND OF SAINT HELENA and its dependencies Tristan da Cunha and Ascension Island make up a British colony in the middle of the south Atlantic Ocean. Saint Helena lies 1,200 miles (1,950 kilometers) west of Angola.

Saint Helena is a volcanic island with an area of just 47 square miles (122 square kilometers). It rises steeply to Diana's Peak, 2,704 feet (824 meters) above sea level.

Tristan da Cunha lies 1,320 miles (2,120 kilometers) farther southwest and is a little smaller than Saint Helena. It is the peak of an active volcano that rises from the seabed to 6,760 feet (2,060 meters) above sea level.

Ascension Island lies 700 miles (1,130 kilometers) northwest of Saint Helena. It is used as a military base and communications center. It has no permanent population.

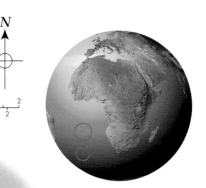

CLIMATE

Saint Helena has a mild climate that varies little throughout the year. Tristan da Cunha has a more varied climate, with a warm, dry season lasting from December to March.

(Saint Helena)
Average January temperature: *80°F (27°C)*
Average July temperature: *70°F (21°C)*
Average annual precipitation: *8 in. (20 cm)*

Far-Flung Islands

Saint Helena (huh-LEE-nuh) and its dependencies were discovered by Portuguese ships in the 1500s C.E., but it was the English East India Company that took possession of Saint Helena in 1659, bringing in English settlers and slaves from Africa as laborers. Coffee was planted in

1732, but Saint Helena's chief value was as a refueling stop for sailing ships. Saint Helena's slaves were liberated between 1818 and 1836. The British government took over Saint Helena from the East India Company in 1834.

In 1870 the opening of the Suez Canal brought about Saint Helena's decline as a port of call. Ships traveling to and from Asia no longer had to pass through south Atlantic waters.

FACTS AND FIGURES

Official name: *Saint Helena and Dependencies*

Status: *British Overseas Territory*

Capital: *Jamestown (on Saint Helena)*

Other town: *Edinburgh (on Tristan da Cunha)*

Area: *133 square miles (345 square kilometers)*

Population: *6,000*

Population density: *45 per square mile (17 per square kilometer)*

Peoples: *Mixed European-Asian-African descent*

Official language: *English*

Currency: *Saint Helena pound*

National day: *Saint Helena Day (May 21)*

Country's name: *It is assumed that Saint Helena was discovered on the saint's feast day, May 21, in 1502. Tristan da Cunha is named after the Portuguese admiral who discovered the island in 1506.*

Helena, but the market collapsed. Coffee is still produced, and frozen tuna fish are also exported. The islands make some money from selling postage stamps, popular with collectors, and in making handicrafts.

Tristan da Cunha has a tightly knit farming community of about three hundred people. They grow potatoes, corn, and green vegetables and herd cattle and sheep on the volcano's slopes. A factory processes catches of crayfish, or rock lobster.

People on both islands are of mixed European (mostly British), Asian, and African descent. All speak English. They are mostly Protestants, members of the Anglican Church. Children go to school between the ages of five and fifteen, and there is a hospital on each of the two islands. In recent years, poverty and unemployment have caused hardship and a feeling that the people are neglected by the British government.

Saint Helena's Girl Guides salute the British Governor as they march past the Court House in Jamestown on Remembrance Sunday, which commemorates the end of both World Wars.

Remote Tristan da Cunha (TRIS-tuhn duh KOO-nyuh) had attracted one or two settlers as early as 1810, and a garrison of British troops was posted to this island in 1815. One soldier stayed on Tristan and founded a permanent colony that passing seafarers joined over the years. Tristan was completely evacuated in 1961 because of a volcanic eruption, but within two years many islanders returned.

Although the islanders now govern themselves, Great Britain pays for about two-third of the islands' budget. The islands' economy is fragile. Flax, for making rope and twine, used to be grown on Saint

Time line:	Islands discovered by Portuguese	English East India Company takes over Saint Helena	Saint Helena becomes British colony	Volcano erupts; Tristan da Cunha evacuated	Television arrives on Saint Helena
	1500s C.E.	1659	1834	1961–1963	1995

SÃO TOMÉ AND PRÍNCIPE

THESE TWO SMALL GREEN ISLANDS LIE IN THE GULF OF GUINEA. Along with a few nearby islets, they make up Africa's second smallest independent country.

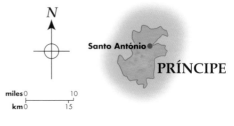

The islands are part of a submerged volcanic ridge that stretches westward from Cameroon. São Tomé lies just over a mile (2 kilometers) north of the equator. It rises to an altitude of 6,639 feet (2,024 meters) at São Tomé Peak. The vegetation is lush and green. Príncipe is a much flatter island, about 90 miles (145 kilometers) to the northeast.

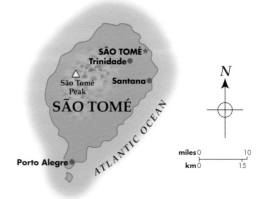

CLIMATE

The islands are hot and humid but are cooled to some extent by ocean currents. The wet season stretches between October and May. The heaviest rainfall is on the mountain slopes of São Tomé.

Average January temperature: *79°F (26°C)*

Average July temperature: *75°F (24°C)*

Average annual precipitation: *38 in. (97 cm)*

In the Gulf of Guinea

Tropical islands where no human has ever set foot are hard to find in modern times, but in the fifteenth century C.E., many such islands were being discovered. In 1470 Portuguese navigators came across a lush, volcanic island in the southeastern Gulf of Guinea (GIH-nee). They called it São Tomé (SOW too-MAE), and in the following year they discovered another island lying to the northeast, which they called Príncipe (PREEN-see-pee).

In 1485 the Portuguese returned to São Tomé to plant sugarcane. They encouraged Portuguese, Spanish, and French people to settle. Many settlers were Jews who had been forced to convert to Christianity back in Europe. Príncipe was settled in 1500. Convict labor and slaves imported from the African mainland worked the plantations. The slave plantations of São Tomé and Príncipe were the first of their kind, becoming the economic model for Brazil and, later, for the Caribbean islands. In the mid-sixteenth century, São Tomé and Príncipe became officially recognized as possessions of Portugal.

The European colonists faced a struggle. Many African slaves escaped and hid in the mountains. In 1530 slaves rose up in rebellion, and many Portuguese were forced to flee to their other territories, such as Brazil. Eventually, however, the Portuguese regained control. Then the sugar trade, which had briefly led the world, rapidly declined in the face of competition from Brazil. From the 1590s the islands were used chiefly as a depot and supply base for the transatlantic slave trade.

During the 1800s coffee was planted and soon became the chief crop. Slavery was not formally abolished until 1875, much later than elsewhere in Africa. Even then, it effectively continued into the 1900s. The contract workers who replaced the slaves had few rights and their harsh lives

FACTS AND FIGURES

Official name: *República Democratica de São Tomé e Príncipe*

Status: *Independent state*

Capital: *São Tomé*

Other towns: *Trindade, Santo António*

Area: *372 square miles (963 square kilometers)*

Population: *160,000*

Population density: *430 per square mile (166 per square kilometer)*

Peoples: *90 percent Fang and other African peoples; 10 percent Mestiços (mixed Portuguese-African descent)*

Official language: *Portuguese*

Currency: *Dobra*

National day: *Independence Day (July 12)*

Country's name: *The name is Portuguese for "Saint Thomas and Prince" Islands.*

resembled those of slaves. In the 1890s cacao trees were planted, to be processed into cocoa, on plantations owned by a small elite of rich Portuguese. This soon became the most important crop, but the world was beginning to take note of the wretched working

The children of workers play outside the old Portuguese colonial buildings of a roça (ROE-sah), a large cocoa plantation, in the steamy highlands of São Tomé.

Time line:	Portuguese, Spanish, and French settle the islands, importing slaves	Slave uprising	Sugar trade declines; islands become refueling point for transatlantic slave trade	Slavery formally abolished	Workers come from other Portuguese colonies
	1485 c.e.	1530	1590s–1600s	1875	1910

conditions on the islands, and many chocolate manufacturers refused to buy cocoa from São Tomé.

After 1910, men from other Portuguese colonies such as Angola and Cape Verde were taken on as indentured workers. Their working conditions were almost as bad as those of the former slaves, and most islanders remained poverty-stricken.

Portugal itself was run by the military beginning in 1926 and by a right-wing dictatorship from 1933 until 1974. This harsh regime led to growing resentment in the islands. After 1953, when Portuguese troops gunned down and killed 1,032 striking plantation workers in what became known as the Batépa Massacre, resentment became more acute and led to the formation of an independence movement.

Working toward Independence

Seven years later, a political party called the Committee for the Liberation of São Tomé and Príncipe (CLSTP) was founded. In 1972 the committee became known as the Movement, or the MLSTP.

The Portuguese dictatorship suddenly ended in 1974. The new Portuguese government at first refused to deal with the MLSTP. However, widespread strikes and a mutiny in the army caused many Portuguese to flee the islands and persuaded the Portuguese government to change its position. São Tomé and Príncipe achieved independence in 1975.

The first president was Manuel Pinto da Costa of the MLSTP. Faced with a threatened coup by right-wing forces,

Angola, Guinea-Bissau, and Cuba sent troops or offered assistance. The plantations were nationalized, and the country became a one-party socialist state.

During the 1980s economic problems in São Tomé and Príncipe mounted. In 1990 the MLSTP moved away from socialist policies, and in 1991 multiparty elections were held. Miguel Trovoada, a former MLSTP member running as an independent, became president. He was reelected in 1996. The MLSTP holds a majority of seats in parliament, which, unusual for a country in Africa, is elected every four years by proportional representation. The government in parliament (since 1999) is led by Prime Minister Guilherme Posser da Costa of the MLSTP.

Island Life

São Tomé and Príncipe are crippled by heavy debts and unemployment is very high. Only aid from the European Union keeps the islands functioning. There are no mineral resources and very limited industry. At the moment most oil has to be imported from Angola. The islands produce soap, textiles, bricks, processed foods, beer, and soft drinks. A tourist industry has begun to attract international visitors in the last fifteen years, and there are plans to develop a duty-free zone on Príncipe in order to attract more visitors.

The islands' chief resource is their fertile, volcanic soil; farmland occupies 54 percent of the total land area. Coffee and cocoa plantations are being upgraded and still represent the chief exports. However, care

1,032 strikers shot dead by Portuguese troops; start of independence movement	Unrest; many Portuguese flee	Independence; industries nationalized	Multiparty elections; Miguel Trovoada becomes president	MLSTP wins a majority in parliament
1953	**1974**	**1975**	**1991**	**1994 and 1999**

Ripe corn cobs are collected from tall plants on the island of São Tomé. Cornmeal is a common and nutritious part of the local diet.

is being taken not to depend too much on any one crop. Copra (dried coconut), palm kernels, corn, bananas, pineapples, and melons are also produced.

The buildings in the small towns and on the old plantations are mostly in Portuguese style and date back to the colonial age. They have whitewashed or colored walls, red tile roofs, and wooden verandas.

Local meals include typically African fare—bananas and plantains, cassava, and cornmeal. Portuguese-style cooking, with plenty of fish dishes, may also be sampled in restaurants. Seafood is widely eaten and includes squid and shellfish as well as a wide range of locally caught fish, such as barracuda. Meat is served in small pastries as a snack. Large amounts of foods always had to be imported, although efforts are being made to grow more crops for local consumption.

The health care system is better than in many African countries. Life expectancy is sixty-two years for men and sixty-six years for women. The chief medical problems are cerebral malaria, an often fatal disease carried by mosquitoes, and respiratory illnesses, such as pneumonia. Eighty-one children in every one thousand die before they are five.

Education is compulsory for all children between the ages of six and twelve, but many adults have had little formal schooling. About 85 percent of men and 62 percent of women can read and write; the difference reflects the old-fashioned view common in Africa that a boy's education is more important than a girl's.

The Portuguese brought their Roman Catholic Christianity with

A mother pays for medicine for her sick child at an outdoor health clinic. Children in São Tomé receive better health care than in many mainland areas of western Africa.

427

Who's Who on the Islands?

The complex history of São Tomé and Príncipe is reflected in the names used to describe the origins of many islanders.

- **Mestiços** *(mehs-TEE-zoez) means people of mixed African-European (mostly Portuguese) descent.*

- **Filhos da Terra** *(FEEL-yoes da TAER-rah) means "sons of the earth" and is another word used to describe Mestiços.*

- **Forros** *(FOE-roesh) means descendants of slaves freed from the plantations when slavery was abolished.*

- **Angolares** *(ahn-goe-LAH-reesh) means descendants of Angolan slaves who were shipwrecked on the islands in 1540. They set up independent fishing villages around the coast.*

- **Serviçais** *(sehr-vih-SIESH) means migrant workers from Angola, Cape Verde, or Mozambique.*

- **Tongas** *(TAWN-gash) means children of Serviçais born on the islands.*

them to the islands, while the African slaves held their own beliefs in the spirit world. Today 81 percent of the islanders are Catholic, while the rest are mostly Protestant, belonging to Africa-based churches or the Seventh-Day Adventists.

A Coming Together of Peoples

Many islanders are of mixed Portuguese-African descent, but the majority of islanders are of solely African origin. Most are descendants either of slaves or of the indentured workers brought from Portugal's other African colonies nearly one hundred years ago.

The official language of São Tomé and Príncipe is Portuguese, but just a few thousand speak it as a first language, and only about half of the islanders are literate in Portuguese. The great majority of the population speak a language known as Gulf of Guinea Creole, or Crioulou (kree-OO-loo), which is based upon old-fashioned Portuguese mixed with various

A fishing boat is hauled up onto a São Tomé beach. The island's fishing communities were founded by shipwrecked slaves and their descendants.

Bantu languages. São Tomé and Príncipe Creole has three main dialects. These reveal the geographical origins of the islanders on mainland Africa, showing the influence of the Kwa languages of the Guinea coast as well as languages of central and southern Africa.

The islands have a long history of dance, drumming, music, and performance, in which Portuguese folk music has fused

A market is held on a São Tomé beach, offering fresh fish straight from the boats and small quantities of homegrown fruits and vegetables.

with African rhythms, as has happened in Brazil. The spectacular *congo* (KAWN-goe) dance is based upon Portuguese and African folktales. Today's pop music style owes more to central Africa than Portugal, with melodies picked out on tinkling electric guitars.

Charlemagne Comes to Africa

Twelve hundred years ago a Frankish king named Charlemagne lived in Europe. He headed an empire that included France, Germany, and northern Italy and fought the Muslim armies who were invading southern Europe from Morocco. His legendary deeds became the subject of folktales and dramas right across western Europe. During the sixteenth century a play was performed about Charlemagne in

Portugal, and after many years it was brought by seafarers from the Portuguese island of Madeira down to São Tomé. There it was taken up by the Angolares and given a distinctly African flavor. Known as the tchiloli *(chi-LOE-lee), it is still performed today in the open air to a musical accompaniment. The characters are masked and wear old-fashioned Portuguese dress.*

SENEGAL

SENEGAL IS THE WESTERNMOST NATION IN MAINLAND AFRICA.

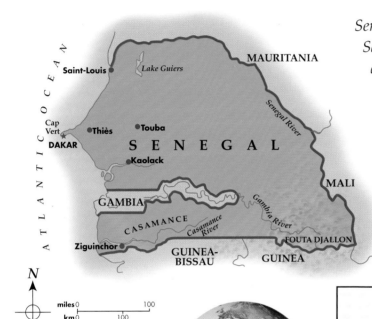

Senegal is mostly flat and low lying. Savanna grasslands and trees cover its dusty red soil. Vegetation grows thickly in the damp south but is sparser in the dry northern half, which is part of the semidesert Sahel. Senegal's major rivers are the Senegal in the north and the Casamance in the south. The Fouta Djallon hills in the southeast are the country's highest point at 1,607 feet (490 meters).

CLIMATE

Compared to nearby countries, Senegal's weather is temperate, especially along the coast. Even in summer, temperatures rarely exceed 95°F (35°C). The southern Casamance region receives almost three times as much rain as the Senegal River Valley in the north. A dry season lasts from November to June, and a wet season from July to October.

Average January temperature: *57°F (14°C)*
Average July temperature: *90°F (32°C)*
Average annual precipitation: *21 in. (53 cm)*

A Fulani woman tends cattle in Casamance in southern Senegal. For hundreds of years people have moved from other parts of western Africa to live in this fertile region.

A Home to Many Peoples

People have found Senegal (seh-nih-GAWL) a good place to live for many thousands of years. Some of the earliest traces of human settlement in western Africa—stone tools and other objects dating from around 13,000 B.C.E.—have been discovered there. However, the first written records of Senegal's history come from the time when Senegal was part of the great Ghana Empire, based in Mali (see MALI), from around 700 to 1000 C.E. During this time the religion of Islam was introduced. After Ghana's power weakened, Senegal was invaded by armies sent by the Berber Almoravid dynasty from Mauritania. The Almoravids were Islamic reformers who strengthened Islam in Senegal.

From around 1200 to 1450, Senegal was part of the powerful Mali Empire (see MALI). During this time groups of Malinke (mah-LING-kae) people arrived in Senegal from other Mali Empire lands. As droughts in the semidesert northern Sahel forced people living there to move south and west in search of food and water, fresh groups of migrants—mostly Serer (seh-REHR), Fulani (foo-LAH-nee), and Tukulor (TOO-koo-loer) families—arrived to settle in Senegal between 1300 and 1500. Meanwhile the Jolof kingdom of the Wolof (WOE-lawf) people became powerful in the central Senegal area. Wolof rulers remained important after 1500, when the Jolof kingdom split up into several smaller states.

The first Europeans reached Senegal in 1445, when Portuguese explorers landed at Cap Vert. They were soon followed by merchants from Portugal, England, and the Netherlands, who purchased slaves from Wolof rulers and sold them to landowners in the Caribbean. European merchants also traded in ivory and gum arabic, a tree resin used to fix dyes in textiles. The French set up a permanent base on Saint-Louis Island in the Senegal River in 1658. In 1670 Muslim leaders based in northern Senegal began a jihad (holy war) against the Wolof slave traders, but the French helped Wolof rulers defeat them.

FACTS AND FIGURES

Official name: République du Sénégal

Status: Independent state

Capital: Dakar

Major town: Thiès, Kaolack, Ziguinchor, Saint-Louis

Area: 76,124 square miles (197,161 square kilometers)

Population: 9,200,000

Population density: 121 per square mile (47 per square kilometer)

Peoples: 36 percent Wolof; 17 percent Fulani; 17 percent Serer and Jola; 9 percent Tukulor; 9 percent Malinke; 1 percent European and Lebanese; 11 percent other

Official language: French

Currency: CFA franc

National days: National Day (April 4); Independence Day (June 20)

Country's name: The name possibly comes from Azanaga, the Portuguese name for the Berber pirates who attacked European ships off the west African coast.

Time line:	First evidence of human settlement	Part of Ghana Empire	Part of Mali Empire	Jolof (Wolof) kingdom grows powerful
	ca. 13,000 B.C.E.	ca. 700–1000 C.E.	ca. 1200–1450	ca. 1300

A Gateway for the French

After powerful European nations banned the international slave trade in 1815, the French began to look for other ways of making money from Senegal. In 1845 they appointed a governor, to be based in Saint-Louis near the coast. He took control of the surrounding lands and forced local people to give up subsistence farming and grow peanuts as a cash crop or work on plantations for wages.

From then on Senegal became a "gateway" for French officials and troops

Senegalese soldiers march ashore in Dahomey, now known as Benin, in 1892. France used its Senegalese army to conquer vast areas of western Africa in the late nineteenth century.

Brave and Skilled Fighters

Many of the Senegalese peoples, especially the Wolof and Fulani, have a long and proud tradition as fighters. French army commanders, who arrived in western Africa during the nineteenth century, admired their bravery and battle skill. They recruited Senegalese troops into the French army, trained them to use the latest European weapons, and appointed African officers to lead them. French Governor Louis-Léon Faidherbe relied on Senegalese soldiers to help him conquer the important Senegal Valley region in the 1850s and 1860s. Later, in the 1880s and 1890s, the French used Senegalese troops to win control of their large west African empire. Senegalese soldiers fought against the Tukulor in Mali and the Malinke in Guinea and led the conquest of Dahomey, now Benin, from 1892 to 1894. Many men from Senegal and neighboring western African countries were also recruited to fight for France against Germany on the battlefields of Europe during World War I (1914–1918).

Arrival of Serer, Fulani, and Tukulor peoples	Portuguese land on coast	Wolof trade with Portuguese, English, and Dutch	French set up colony at Saint-Louis Island	Muslim war against French and Wolof slave traders	Europeans ban slave trade
ca. 1300–1500	1445	ca. 1500–1650	1658	1670s	1815

trying to take control of other parts of western Africa farther inland. They moved up the Senegal River Valley in the 1850s and 1860s, and from 1879 to 1881 they extended their conquests toward Mali. Many Senegalese peoples fiercely opposed the growing French power, especially the Muslim marabouts (religious leaders) and their allies, the Wolof chiefs. In 1885 the European powers defined the boundaries of French territory to include Senegal.

In 1887 literate and wealthy Africans living in the four largest towns in Senegal were given limited French citizenship, and during the early twentieth century, a few members of elite African families went to schools and universities in France and began to play a small part in French politics. However, most Senegalese did not have civil rights or the chance of an education. They were simply expected to work for, and obey, their French colonial masters. From around 1914 African leaders such as Blaise Diagne (the first black member of the French National Assembly) and Amadou Lamine Guèye (Africa's first black lawyer) campaigned for better treatment for native Senegalese.

Like other people in western Africa, the inhabitants of Senegal began to demand independence from France shortly before the end of World War II (1939–1945). The most powerful Senegalese campaigner, Léopold Senghor, suggested that the former French colonies in western Africa should join together after independence to strengthen their dealings with foreign powers. He planned a "super-state," to be known as the Mali Federation. This was formed in 1959 by Senegal and Mali but lasted only a short time since other African leaders did not fully support it. It broke up in 1960, the year that Senegal became independent.

The First Years of Independence

Senghor became the first president of independent Senegal. His political views were fairly conservative, supporting African nationalism but also favoring close ties with France. His own political party, the Socialist Party, was the only one allowed, but people with different views were allowed to discuss them in public and to criticize the government—unusual political freedoms at that time in western Africa.

However, the economic outlook was poor. Senegal had few industries or natural resources. In 1967 the French government abolished its subsidy to peanut farmers. Peanuts were Senegal's main crop, so this led to serious economic problems. In 1968 antipoverty riots and protests by students and trade unions arose but were suppressed with the aid of French troops. In 1974 Senghor agreed to democratic reforms, including multiparty elections.

In 1980 Senghor volunteered to retire because of his age. He named Vice President Abdou Diouf as his chosen successor, believing that Diouf would continue his policies. However, Diouf introduced more democratic reforms and led an anticorruption campaign, during which many of Senghor's old colleagues

French attempt to conquer Senegal	Senegal recognized as French colony	Independence campaigns	Federation with Mali	Independence; Léopold Senghor first president	Economic problems lead to riots
1845–1880s	1885	1940s–1950s	1959–1960	1960	1968

were fired. Diouf also became actively involved in international affairs. In the summer of 1981, he was asked by the Gambian government to help put down a coup. He sent troops and agreed with Gambian plans for uniting their two countries. The Senegambia Confederation was formed in 1982.

Conflict Abroad and at Home

Diouf was reelected president in 1983, but the next round of elections, in 1988, led to a fresh crisis. Opposition leader Abdoulaye Wade was imprisoned, then sent into exile. When his supporters protested, Diouf ordered army tanks to patrol the streets. After the election results were announced, people in Senegal and abroad accused Diouf and his supporters of vote rigging. The following year, the political situation worsened as the Senegambia Confederation collapsed. After a dispute over grazing rights, fighting began on the northern border with Mauritania, leading to riots in Senegal and Mauritania. Many people on both sides were killed, and thousands of Senegalese living in Mauritania were driven from their homes and deported. In return the Senegalese government expelled all Mauritanians living in Senegal.

At the same time people living in the agricultural southern Casamance (kah-zah-MAHS) region rebelled. Casamance produces rice for the whole country, but Casamance's non-Muslim Jola (JOE-lah) majority felt ignored by Senegal's Muslim-led government. Rebels wanting

independence for Casamance attacked government buildings and killed Senegalese soldiers and officials. An uneasy cease-fire was announced in 1991, but this broke down the next year, and sporadic fighting between government troops and rebels continued throughout the decade.

In 1990 opposition leader Wade returned from exile. He called for a change in government policies and a chance for all democratic political parties to have a share in government. In 1991 Wade was made minister of state but had little real power.

By 1993 the years of war and unrest had led to serious economic problems, made worse by the collapse of the tourist industry in Casamance. To save money, the government cut wages and public services. This led to riots and strikes, and Wade was arrested for supporting the protesters. In 1994 there were further economic reforms, backed by international aid donors. New private businesses (many specializing in telecommunications) were encouraged; they succeeded, and this led to economic growth. France urged peace between Wade and Diouf, and as a result Wade and six of his political allies received positions in the government. This brought some political stability, although the government still faced political unrest in the Casamance region.

Wade was elected president in March 2000, when his Democratic Party of Senegal won 58 percent of the vote. Diouf immediately conceded defeat and stepped down peacefully. His Socialist Party had ruled Senegal since independence.

Abdou Diouf becomes president	Senegambia Confederation	Dispute with Mauritania; rebellion begins in Casamance	Serious economic problems; economic reforms; development of communications industry	Abdoulaye Wade elected president
1980	**1982–1989**	**1989**	**1990s**	**2000**

This Wolof man is wearing a headdress to protect himself from windblown dust and sand. The Wolof dominate the area in the north around the capital, Dakar.

Senegal's Peoples

Over the centuries many different peoples have migrated to live in Senegal. Today the Wolof people of the northern and central regions form the largest and most influential group in Senegal. Since the 1980s they have held most of the important jobs in government and business and have been accused by other groups of favoring the Wolof language and social customs and neglecting all other groups.

For hundreds of years the Wolof people were divided into several different castes, according to birth. Nobles and warriors had the highest rank; next came farmers and traders. Artisans, musicians, and storytellers had low social status but were admired and respected for their skills. Slaves had the lowest rank of all.

Today these customs are changing; education and a well-paying or influential job give power to individual Wolof men and women, whatever their birth, and low-caste Wolof musicians earn fame and riches. Slavery is banned by law, although the descendants of former slaves often work as laborers and poor farmers on rich families' lands.

However, many Wolof people still follow long-established social customs. For example, nobles are always expected to

Today many Senegalese women follow professional careers, such as this teacher who is instructing a class in basic reading and writing. The words on the blackboard are in the Wolof language.

435

show courage and self-control, to present a dignified image in public, and to never bring shame to their families. Wolof men and women have long been admired by other Senegalese people for their good looks and elegant clothes. Wolof women, in particular, have always worn elaborate headdresses, lots of jewelry, and dramatic flowing robes. Today Wolof people set the fashion trends for all of Senegal.

The Fulani and the Tukulor also live in the north. Both are expert cattle herders; the Tukulor also fish along the banks of the Senegal River. In recent years many Tukulor people have moved to live in cities because their grazing land has dried up and become desert. Fulani and Tukulor society is divided into castes of nobles, farmers and cattle keepers, artisans, and slaves. Male

Brightly dressed women prepare food, chat, and look after their children in a tree-shaded village in Casamance. Many women here also work as traders in local markets.

elders from the noble caste head the villages or bands of nomadic herders.

In contrast, the Jola people of the Casamance region in the south are organized into family-based clans, with fewer differences in rank between people with different occupations or skills. Heads of clans (always men) command loyalty from other members, who are very proud of their lineage and clan name. Many Jola live in towns as merchants and artisans. Men and women both take part in trade. Only men can weave cloth, but the thread they use is spun by women.

The Serer people also live in the south. They are farmers, growing rice and millet and raising cattle, sheep, and goats. Like the Jola, they base their society on clans but trace their family membership through women, not men. A man can have several wives, and each has her own household, where she raises her children. Villages of

these households are ruled by local chiefs and councils, who are all male.

The Malinke have lived close to the Serer and ruled them for many centuries. Some Malinke are farmers, others find work in towns. Their society is also organized around clans. Men may have several wives, so long as they can pay the necessary bride prices to their wives' fathers.

Language and Religion

French is the official language of Senegal, but it is spoken only by the well-educated minority. Each of the different peoples has their own language, but many also speak

Brotherhoods

Muslim brotherhoods are one of the most remarkable features of life in Senegal. While almost all Muslim men belong to one of the five brotherhoods, women cannot join. The brotherhoods originated hundreds of years ago for religious and charitable purposes. Today they play an influential part in politics, control many profitable businesses, and shape the way that ordinary people think. The most powerful are the Mouridiya (moo-REED-yah), who support the present government, and the Tidjanes (tee-JAH-neez), whom some politicians accuse of planning a revolution to set up a completely Islamic state. Each brotherhood is led by a marabout (MAH-rah-boo)—a religious teacher—who gives orders to his followers and expects complete obedience from them.

Wolof, which is used as a common tongue. Muslim scholars and religious teachers also speak Arabic, the holy language of Islam. The Muslim greeting, "Peace be with you," is used by ordinary people of all faiths. Along the coast people speak Kriyol (Creole), a mixture of Portuguese and various African languages originally used by merchants and sailors.

Over 90 percent of the population is Muslim, although the teachings of Islam are often mixed with local beliefs in spirits,

Delicate plasterwork decorates the main gateway to this Muslim mosque in Dakar. The worshipers, all men, come here every Friday to listen to a sermon.

437

The Magal Pilgrimage

Once a year, about half a million pilgrims flock to the city of Touba, Senegal's holiest shrine. They come to pray at the tomb of Amadou Bamba, a Wolof prince born in the nineteenth century. Bamba was a powerful marabout, a Muslim religious teacher. In 1887 he founded the Mouridiya (Hopeful) Muslim brotherhood. At first its members fought fiercely against the French colonial rulers of Senegal; later Bamba encouraged them to work hard in the peanut fields and create wealth for Wolof leaders.

Bamba's tomb is housed in a huge mosque, which towers 285 feet (87 meters) high above the surrounding city and plains. Touba itself is a center of Muslim scholarship and home of the Grand Marabout (senior religious leader). It is ruled by Muslim law and even has its own Muslim police force.

people farm depends on where they live. In the dry, dusty northern and central regions, the Wolof homelands, peanuts are the main crop. They are sold to merchants, and the money is used to buy clothes and household goods. Wolof farmers also grow sorghum and millet as food for their families and plant beans, peppers, okra, and tomatoes in garden plots. The Fulani and Tukulor also grow grains, peanuts, and cotton, but some Fulani continue their traditional way of life as nomadic cattle herders. Farther south, where the land is wetter and the climate warmer, Jola and Serer farmers grow rice, fruits, and vegetables in flooded fields beside the Casamance River.

Village houses can be either square or circular but are usually made of mud or sun-dried mud bricks and roofed with thatch or metal sheets. They consist of several separate rooms built around a

Mud-brick houses thatched with dried grass in a Tukulor village on the edge of the desert in northern Senegal. The wooden fence in the foreground is part of a cattle enclosure.

magic healing, and fetishes (protective charms). Different groups of peoples have different faiths. The Wolof, Malinke, Fulani, and Tukulor are mostly Muslim, some Serer are Christian, while many Jola follow African religions.

Living in the Country

Although less than one-third of the Senegalese land is suitable for growing crops, almost four out of every five people in Senegal earn their living by farming. How

A group of boys plays in a village square. Country children make their own wheeled toys out of pieces of wire, used cans, and plastic bottles.

central courtyard; often, each compound (collection of rooms) is surrounded by a wall. Wolof villages are usually large, with homes for several hundred people. Other villages may be smaller; for example, each Malinke village houses members of just one clan. Most villages have a public square in the center, used for dancing and wrestling, Senegal's most popular sport. A mosque stands in Muslim villages.

Towns and Industries

In coastal towns and cities like Dakar (dah-KAHR), Senegal's capital, many old European-style homes still stand. They were built for French governors and officials during the colonial era, and they were surrounded by lush gardens. Today many of these homes are occupied by rich and powerful Senegalese. Less wealthy citizens live in a mixture of high-rise apartment buildings, small mud-brick or concrete houses with tin roofs, and run-down French colonial-style houses with courtyards, terra-cotta-tiled roofs, and whitewashed walls. Dakar faces fast-growing problems of unemployment, homelessness, juvenile delinquency, and drug abuse.

Dakar is a major port, with one of the few good natural harbors in western Africa. It is the center of Senegal's fishing and fish-canning industry. Fish (especially tuna and shrimp) and peanuts are Senegal's two most important exports. Dakar's port also handles bulk cargoes of phosphates and fertilizers and has gas refineries.

Many new telecommunications businesses have sprung up in the 1990s, and Senegal's telephone system has been modernized. The country is a center of

Boys in Dakar play table soccer in front of a telecenter, an office where anyone can pay a small fee to make a telephone call or send a fax.

international communications and home to the Pan-African News Agency. There are several radio and TV stations, and people can receive French satellite television. A growing number of multinational computer-based businesses are setting up in Senegal.

Senegal's other industries are not well developed. Only tourism brings considerable income to the country.

National Dishes

Few people in Senegal go hungry, although most cannot afford luxuries. Even so, Senegalese cooks are famous for preparing some of the best food in Africa. Dishes in Senegal are usually composed of a starchy food, such as rice or millet, plus a tasty sauce. *Tcheboudienne* (cheh-BOOD-yehn), the national dish, consists of boiled rice with a thick sauce made of fish baked with vegetables and spices, topped with tomatoes and peppers. *Riz jollof* (REEZ-joe-lawf), or rice with chicken or vegetables cooked in palm oil, is another national favorite. Rice may also be served with okra or peanut sauces. *Bassi-salété* (BAH-see sah-LAE-tuh), millet with meat and vegetables, is eaten on special occasions such as births, weddings, national holidays, and at community and religious festivals.

In towns, shops sell French-style bread, baked from wheat, and restaurants serve French and Lebanese meals and snacks such as *charwarma* (SHWAHR-muh), slices of meat kebab wrapped in bread. Desserts are not widely eaten, although some tropical fruits are grown in the warm, moist south.

Poulet Yassa

Poulet yassa (poo-LAY YAH-suh) is a popular dish throughout western Africa, but in Senegal it's particularly associated with the Casamance region. It uses produce—lemons and peppers—that grows in areas with good rainfall.

You will need:

> *4 large pieces of chicken*
> *nearly 1 pound (400 grams) of onions, finely sliced in rings*
> *4 red or green sweet peppers, chopped and with seeds removed*
> *1 small mild chili, chopped and with seeds removed*
> *10 cloves of garlic, chopped*
> *2 bay leaves*
> *1 tablespoon (15 grams) flour*
> *1/2 teaspoon (2.5 grams) black pepper*
> *1/2 teaspoon (2.5 grams) salt*
> *1 large lemon*
> *2 tablespoons (30 milliliters) cooking oil*
> *1 1/2 cups (.35 liters) water or chicken stock*

Squeeze juice from one lemon. Pour it over chicken pieces and leave them in the refrigerator for two hours.

Coat chicken pieces in flour. Heat oil in heavy saucepan. Fry chicken pieces gently in oil until golden brown all over. Add all other ingredients. Cover pan and stew gently until chicken is tender. Add more water if needed; mixture should be fairly thick.

Serve with boiled rice, sliced tomatoes, and lemon wedges.

This quantity serves four people.

A Fulani family cooks a meal of couscous—tiny, fluffy grains of dried wheat—on an outdoor fire. Away from towns and cities, few Senegalese homes have indoor kitchens.

Southern farmers also gather wild fruits from the forests to sell at local markets.

Popular drinks include local beer, *kinkilaba* (keen-kee-LAH-bah), which is an herb tea, *bissap* (BEE-sahp), a cool, refreshing drink made from hibiscus flowers, and sharp-tasting juice from baobab trees. Southerners enjoy palm wine made from the sap of palm trees, and northerners like hot sweet tea.

Health and Education

The moderate climate makes Senegal a fairly healthy place to live, and during the 1980s and 1990s the government introduced policies designed to improve

Tabaski: A National Celebration

Every year Muslims throughout the world celebrate the Feast of the Sacrifice. It commemorates the time (recorded in Muslim, Jewish, and Christian traditions) when the prophet Abraham offered his beloved only son, Isaac, as a sacrifice to God. God commanded Abraham to let his son live and to sacrifice a sheep instead.

In Senegal and other western African countries, the Feast of the Sacrifice is known as Tabaski *(tuh-BASH-kee) and is an important public holiday. Every family who can afford it kills and cooks a sheep, inviting friends and relatives to enjoy the feast and giving a share of the meat and other foods to the poor.*

health care. As a result, a boy born today can expect to live for about fifty-one years, and a girl can expect to live fifty-four years. However, some problems persist. Malaria (a parasite carried by mosquitoes) is common, as is AIDS.

Over the past twenty years the government has opened schools and trained more teachers, but these improvements have not yet led to widespread improvements in literacy. Almost half the men over age fifteen can read and write, but only about one-quarter of the women are literate. As in many parts of Africa, a lot of families do not consider it worthwhile to educate girls. Even today, not all children go to school. Instead they stay at home to help their families in small businesses or on farms.

This boy attends a Koranic school, where he will learn passages from the Koran, the Islamic holy book, by heart. He will also be taught how to read and write.

Music and Art

The people of Senegal have a rich heritage of music and art. In recent years Senegalese musicians have become famous all over the world. The best-known are Youssou N'Dour and his band, the Super Etoile de Dakar (Dakar Superstars), whose music combines *mbalax* (bah-LASH), fast Wolof drumming, with modern Western styles.

Crafts too are many and varied. Many people weave intricate cotton fabrics and brightly colored batiks, decorated with geometric patterns. In the city of Thiès (TIES), expert weavers create tapestries and wall hangings showing scenes from everyday life. Skilled artisans also produce wood carvings, basketry, leather work, and pottery using long-established techniques. Tukulor artists are famous for their fine wood

Women in colorful robes and head scarves sew clothes for customers at an outdoor market in Dakar. Fashionable women's dresses are long and low necked.

carvings. For centuries Mauritanians living in Dakar have made beautiful silver jewelry and wooden chests with silver decoration. Senegalese jewelers also make fine necklaces and earrings in silver and gold. Many Senegalese artists specialize in *souwers* (SOO-wers), a way of painting on glass. This technique was

imported from Asia in the nineteenth century. Today it is used to create scenes of daily life and portraits of Senegalese heroes. A national festival of glass painting is held every year.

Wolof singer Youssou N'Dour and his band have won worldwide fame. Their music, featuring fast drumming in complicated rhythms, mixes African styles with soul, rock, and jazz.

SEYCHELLES

MAKING UP THE SMALLEST INDEPENDENT NATION IN ALL OF AFRICA, the Seychelles archipelago lies about 600 miles (965 kilometers) northeast of Madagascar in the Indian Ocean.

Ninety percent of the population lives on the largest island, Mahé. The granite Inner Islands surrounding Mahé are mostly lush and green. Coastlines of lagoons and sandy beaches rise to steep hills or mountains of 2,968 feet (905 meters) at Morne Seychellois on Mahé. The coral Outer Islands include the Aldabra, Farquhar, and Amirante chains. These islands are flat, with little fresh water. Few of them are suitable for human settlement.

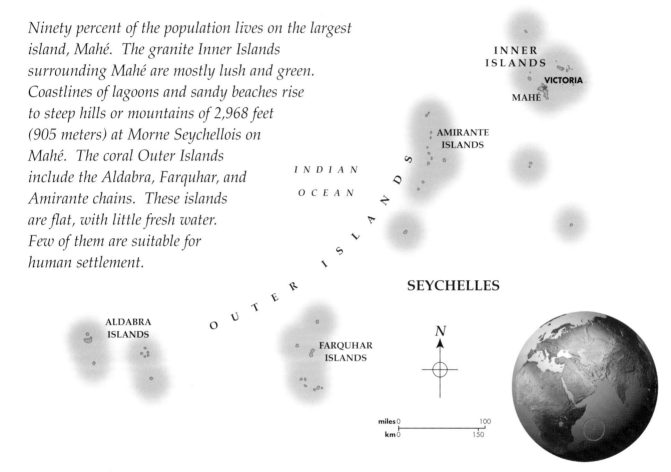

INNER ISLANDS

VICTORIA

MAHÉ

AMIRANTE ISLANDS

INDIAN OCEAN

OUTER ISLANDS

SEYCHELLES

ALDABRA ISLANDS

FARQUHAR ISLANDS

N

miles 0   100
km 0   150

CLIMATE

The islands are humid during the rainy season, which lasts from December to May. From June to November the southeast winds bring cooler weather.

Average January temperature: *80°F (27°C)*
Average July temperature: *78°F (26°C)*
Average annual precipitation: *95 in. (241 cm)*

Turquoise blends with bands of blue across the deepening Indian Ocean. This is a view of Victoria, the capital of Seychelles, on the northern island of Mahé.

444

In the Indian Ocean

Nobody lived on the Seychelles (sae-SHEL) in ancient times. By 1768 C.E. small numbers of French colonists were settling on Mahé (mah-AE). Several hundred African slaves were brought in from other French colonies to plant spices. The islanders also sold timber and tortoise meat to passing ships when they came to stock up on supplies.

In 1794 the British were at war with France. They captured Mahé and did so again in 1806. In 1814 the Treaty of Paris awarded the islands to Great Britain permanently.

Slavery was abolished on the Seychelles in 1835. During the following years freed slaves from eastern Africa and other workers from India and China increased the labor force.

There were no elections until 1948, but even then voting was strictly limited, and the island was dominated by powerful white landowners.

Independence finally came in 1976. James Mancham of the Seychelles Democratic Party became president of the new republic, and France-Albert René of the Seychelles Peoples United Party became his prime minister. The two men were very different. Mancham enjoyed power and wealth, while René was a left-wing radical who called for social change. One year later René ousted Mancham while he was out of the country. René made the Seychelles a one-party state and set up armed forces and militias. Many Europeans decided to leave.

FACTS AND FIGURES

Official name: Republic of the Seychelles

Status: Independent state

Capital: Victoria

Area: 107 square miles (277 square kilometers)

Population: 80,000

Population density: 748 per square mile (289 per square kilometer)

Peoples: 96 percent Creole (mixed African-European descent); 3 percent French or British descent; 1 percent Asian descent

Official language: Kreol

Currency: Seychelles rupee

National day: National Day (June 18)

Country's name: Named in 1756 after Moreau de Séchelles, finance minister of King Louis XV of France. The spelling Seychelles was introduced by the British.

The Seychelles were becoming increasingly dependent on tourism for their survival. René tried to build up agriculture, fisheries, and other industries in order to make a more balanced economy. In 1991, under increasing international pressure for democratic and economic reform, he promised a return to multiparty politics and in 1993 was duly elected president. His renamed party (the Seychelles People's Progressive Front) defeated Mancham's relaunched Democratic Party for the parliament, too. The 1990s proved to be a more peaceful and increasingly prosperous era. By 1998, when René was reelected president, the Seychelles were no longer dependent on foreign aid.

Time line:	French settlers bring in African slaves	Seychelles ceded to Great Britain	Slavery abolished; workers come from India and China	Independence; James Mancham elected president	Coup led by France-Albert René	Multiparty elections; René elected president
	1770s	**1814**	**1835**	**1976**	**1977**	**1993**

The Seychelles Today

Tourism remains the major source of wealth. Since 1996 the island of Mahé has also tried to make itself a center for international business. Industries include chemical, cement, paint, and paper manufacturing, food and drink processing, and oil refining. Tuna fishing and canning is an important export industry. The islands have no mineral resources, and all fuel has to be imported.

Forty-five percent of the islanders live in the countryside. Farmers still grow plants for spices and perfumes. Coconut groves provide copra (dried coconut flesh) for export. Fruits include limes, bananas, mangoes, and guavas. Other local crops include cassava, sugarcane, and sweet potatoes.

The most common basic food, rice, has to be imported. Ocean fish, lobster, squid, and octopus are caught in large numbers. Both fish and chicken are served with rice. Curries are popular, flavored with coconut and spices. *Daube* (DOWB) is a sweet vegetable sauce, and *rougail* (roo-GAE) is a tomato sauce. *Brèdes* (BREHDZ), green spinachlike leaves, are served with many dishes.

The standard of living is high. There is good, free health care, and women can expect to live to seventy-eight years, and men to sixty-nine years. Education is free and compulsory for children between the ages of six and fifteen. Eighty-six percent of men and 82 percent of women can read and write.

One legacy of French rule is the Roman Catholic faith, which was brought by missionaries and today is followed by about 90 percent of the islanders. The Anglican form of Protestant Christianity,

Dressed up for their first communion, young Roman Catholic girls fill the pews of a church at Baie Lazare, in Mahé's southwest.

brought by the British, is followed by about 8 percent of the population.

Attitudes toward family are very relaxed, with marriage playing no important part in Seychelles life. Most children are born outside marriage, taking their mother's first name as their family name.

People and Language

The vast majority of the islanders are of thoroughly mixed descent, part European, part African. They are known as Creoles. There are small communities of people of French, British, Indian, and Chinese descent.

The Seychelles were French for just forty-two years, but the French language and way of life were the most tenacious. Ninety-six percent of all islanders speak a Creole language called Seselwa, which is based on French but also includes words from English, Indian, and African languages of the Bantu group.

A Festival Kreol is held in the Seychelles each October to promote Creole languages

Let's Talk Kreol Seselwa

Kreol Seselwa, the type of Creole spoken on the Seychelles, has been the official language of the islands since 1981. It is similar to dialects spoken on Mauritius.

bonzour *(bon-ZOOR)*	*good day*
azordi *(ah-zoer-DEE)*	*today*
koman ou sava? *(koe-ma-noo-sah-VAH)*	*how are you?*
eski ou kontan? *(skee-oo-coen-TAHN)*	*is that satisfactory?*
lakaz *(lah-KAHZ)*	*house*
bato peser *(bah-TOE-peh-sehr)*	*fishing boat*
gran mersi *(grah-mehr-SEE)*	*many thanks*

and ways of life. Attracting visitors from many parts of the world, it celebrates theater, arts and crafts, literature, fashion, cooking, music, and dance.

The popular music of Mahé is based around the *sega* (SAE-gah), a rhythmic song and dance that is typical of many of Africa's Indian Ocean islands (see MAURITIUS). French heritage can be seen in a lively folk-dance style called the *camtolle* (kam-toe-LAE). Slaves from eastern Africa and Madagascar brought the *sombre moutia* (SAHM-bruh MOOT-yah), a slow song and dance based on chants used when working the plantations. A wide range of folk instruments may be heard, including African-style drums; the *makalapo* (muhk-LAH-poe), which is a stringed instrument; the *bom* (BOEM), played with a bow; and the *zez* (ZEHZ), a stringed instrument like the Indian sitar, or lute.

Women and children help fishermen land a catch on a beach on the island of Mahé. Seafood is a major source of protein for the people of the Seychelles.

SIERRA LEONE

SIERRA LEONE IS A SMALL COUNTRY on the coast of western Africa.

The landscape of Sierra Leone can be divided into three main zones: the marshy, low-lying coast; the rolling central plateau; and the Loma Mountains in the north and northeast. Mangroves and oil palms grow along the coast. Grasslands, woodlands, and farms cover the central region and lush rain forests climb the mountain slopes.

Settlers from around the World

Archaeological evidence so far discovered suggests that hunters and foragers were living in the Sierra Leone (see-EHR-uh lee-OEN) region from about 8000 B.C.E. Over the centuries many different peoples moved into the region and settled. From about 1200 C.E. Mandingo (mahn-DING-goe) people arrived from lands to the northeast. From around this time until 1450, Sierra Leone became part of the mighty Mali Empire, which controlled most of the vast Sahel region (see MALI). The Temne (TEHM-nee) and related peoples were in the area by the early 1400s C.E., having probably come from Fouta Djallon (FOO-tah-JAH-loen) in modern Guinea. Peoples speaking languages of a group called Mande (MAHN-dee) were assimilated into the area through the fifteenth and sixteenth centuries.

CLIMATE

Sierra Leone has a hot, moist, tropical climate. Heavy monsoon rains fall almost every day from May to early November. From December to March the harmattan wind blows in from the Sahara Desert, filling the air with clouds of dust.

Average January temperature: *77°F (25°C)*
Average July temperature: *86°F (30°C)*
Average annual precipitation: *124 in. (315 cm)*

During the 1500s many Portuguese sailors settled in Sierra Leone and married African women. Their descendants became known as the Krio (KREE-oe), and their culture blended African and Portuguese languages and traditions. Krio people became merchants, doing business with both Africans and Portuguese.

Around the same time the international slave trade began, and slaves from Sierra Leone were sent to North America.

FACTS AND FIGURES

Official name: *Republic of Sierra Leone*

Status: *Independent state*

Capital: *Freetown*

Major town: *Koidu*

Area: *27,699 square miles (71,740 square kilometers)*

Population: *5,300,000*

Population density: *191 per square mile (74 per square kilometer)*

Peoples: *39 percent Mande-speakers, including Mende, Susu, Loko, Kono, Kuranko, and Mandingo; 32 percent Temne and related groups; 10 percent Krio (mixed African-European descent); 8 percent Limba and related groups; also Fulani, Lebanese, Indian, and Pakistani*

Official language: *English*

Currency: *Leone*

National days: *Independence Day (April 27); Revolution Day (April 29)*

Country's name: *Sierre Leone means "lion mountain" in Portuguese.*

Freetown to house returning slaves. The freed slaves continued to arrive until the mid-nineteenth century. They mingled with the other inhabitants of Freetown to form another Krio, or Creole, culture.

British Rule

From 1808 Freetown was a colony of Great Britain's and ruled by the British government. Soon the British tried to expand inland from the coast. They signed treaties with local rulers, giving British merchants and soldiers permission to travel and trade. In 1896 Great Britain declared the rest of Sierra Leone to be a protectorate under British guardianship.

British demands for taxes led to a rebellion by Sierra Leone's indigenous peoples, particularly the Temne and Mende (MEHN-dee), in 1898. The war ended in 1899, and Great Britain introduced a

Protests from religious and humanitarian leaders led to the gradual abolition of the slave trade after 1750 and to campaigns for slaves to be freed and returned to their African homelands. During the 1780s freed Africans and British humanitarians founded the city of

Freetown, the capital city of Sierra Leone, photographed around 1900. At that time many streets were unpaved and lined with village-style houses made of wood, mud brick, and thatch.

Time line:	Earliest evidence of human settlement	Mandingo people arrive from northeast	Sierra Leone part of Mali Empire	Ancestors of Temne-speaking peoples arrive from north
	ca. 8000 B.C.E.	ca. 1200 C.E.	ca. 1200–1450	ca. 1400s

449

system of indirect rule through local chiefs, which created over one hundred tiny chiefdoms. The system encouraged rivalry rather than cooperation between the groups, weakening any opposition to the British. Unlike the Krio colony of Freetown, which was ruled separately, inhabitants of these states had no chance of education or good jobs. Neither they nor the Krio people had equal civil rights with the British settlers.

Independence and Corruption

Great Britain's attitude to the lands it ruled in Africa began to change after World War II (1939–1945). Soldiers from Sierra Leone had served in the British army and air force. They could no longer be treated as second-class citizens when they returned home. In 1947 a new constitution gave Africans from outside of Freetown a majority of seats in Sierra Leone's Legislative Council. Meanwhile Africans formed the Sierra Leone People's Party, which won a large majority in Legislative Council elections in 1951. Gradually People's Party members took over many important administrative posts.

In 1961 Sierra Leone was granted independence and Freetown was joined to the rest of the country. Sir Milton Margai (a Mende) became prime minister. He encouraged peace, stability, and national unity.

Sir Milton died in 1964, and his younger brother, Albert Margai, took over. In the 1967 elections Margai was opposed by Siaka Stevens, leader of the All Peoples Congress, which drew its main support from the Limba (LEEM-bah) and Temne people in the north. Stevens was declared the winner, but before he could take power, Margai's supporters in the army staged a coup. However, in 1968 civilian rule was restored and Stevens became prime minister. He turned Sierra Leone into a one-party state. During Stevens' rule, massive corruption among government ministers and officials seriously weakened the economy.

In 1985 Major General Joseph Momoh, the army leader, was elected president. International aid donors demanded major changes to government policies. This led to a severe economic crisis, as ministers were forced to admit that the country was almost bankrupt.

The Years of War

In 1990 the political crisis deepened when Momoh sent Sierra Leone troops to join the Economic Community (of West African States) Monitoring Group (ECOMOG), a peacekeeping force from several western African countries, which was trying to end the Liberian civil war across Sierra Leone's southern border (see LIBERIA). In retaliation, in 1991 the Liberian guerrilla leader Charles Taylor invaded Sierra Leone. At the same time the antigovernment Revolutionary United Front (RUF) protesters based in the eastern part of the country seized their chance to rebel, demanding an end to government corruption and better conditions and wages for the army. Diamond smugglers also stirred up the conflict as a cover for their activities.

Mande-speaking peoples arrive	Portuguese sailors settle	Thousands of slaves shipped to Americas	Freed slaves arrive from Europe, the United States, and the Caribbean	Freetown becomes colony of Great Britain
ca. 1400–1600	1500s	ca. 1550–1750	1787–1850s	1808

The government's army was made up mostly of undisciplined recruits from lawless city slums. Instead of fighting the Liberians or the RUF rebels, they raided and looted ordinary people in their own homes and turned against Momoh himself.

In 1992 a group of army officers overthrew Momoh's government. Although they tried to improve the economy, corruption and diamond smuggling continued, and out-of-control soldiers still terrorized ordinary people. In 1994 a group of traditional Sierra Leone

Armed with guns, these local hunters stand ready to defend their village during the civil war that troubled Sierra Leone for most of the 1990s.

leaders (chiefs and heads of secret societies) tried to bring peace in their own way. They set up private armies to restore law and order.

In 1996 a civilian government was elected. Ahmad Tejan Kabbah became the new president, but in May 1997 he was overthrown in an army coup.

Other western African nations were now worried about the stability of their region. So ECOMOG forces, led by Nigeria, moved in. In October 1997 ECOMOG arranged a cease-fire between the government and the rebels and made plans for a return to democratic rule. However, in February 1998 the cease-fire broke down. Rebel

Great Britain declares Sierra Leone a protectorate	Rebellion against British	Sierra Leone People's Party wins majority on Legislative Council	Independence; Sir Milton Margai becomes prime minister
1896	**1898–1899**	**1951**	**1961**

armies reached Freetown and were barely held back. In March 1998 President Kabbah returned from exile.

In January 1999 the rebels attacked Freetown again. This attack was brought to an end in May 1999, after weeks of destruction and brutality. An uneasy cease-fire was agreed among the warring groups in Sierra Leone, and international agencies appealed for urgent aid. They warned that a major humanitarian crisis might develop unless peace could be maintained and food, shelter, and medicines could be supplied.

Sierra Leone is still a very dangerous place. Government troops and police cannot control all the different armies, warlords, bandits, and armed gangs of smugglers still active there. The struggle for control of the country's diamond production by many of the factions involved has been a major reason the conflict has continued for so long.

The Peoples of Sierra Leone

Over twenty different ethnic groups live in Sierra Leone. The two largest groups are the Mande—that is, speakers of the Mande family of languages, including the Mende, Mandingo, Susu (SOO-soo), Loko (LOE-koe), Kono (KOE-noe), and Kuranko (koo-RAHN-koe) peoples—and the Temne. Together they make up more than two-thirds of the population. Smaller groups

Frightened and exhausted, refugees from Sierra Leone's civil war arrive at a camp on the outskirts of Freetown, carrying their belongings in sacks.

include the Limba, the Fulani (foo-LAH-nee), and the Krio. There are also small communities of Lebanese, Indians, and Pakistanis, traders and businesspeople who arrived between the 1880s and the mid-twentieth century. In the late 1980s and early 1990s, a large number of refugees fleeing civil war in Liberia increased Sierra Leone's population.

English is the official language of Sierra Leone, but it is spoken only by government officials and the educated elite. All the different peoples speak their own local languages. Almost everyone uses Krio as the language of business.

Most of the Mande-speakers in the south follow African beliefs in nature spirits and in honoring ancestors, although a few are Christian and a small minority are Muslim.

Corruption and inefficiency under Siaka Stevens	Joseph Momoh plans economic and political reforms but is overthrown	Sierra Leone intervenes in Liberian Civil War	Liberia invades Sierra Leone	Civil war
1968–1985	**1985–1992**	**1990**	**1991**	**1991–2000**

Mande language, but their culture is different from other Mande-speakers. They are organized in clans, large family groups claiming descent from a single ancestor. Each clan claims one species of animal sacred to it. The animal acts as a symbol of identity and is believed to protect the clan, endowing it with strength and power. Clan members refuse to eat their sacred species.

The Temne, from the north, are mainly Muslim. Like other savanna-dwelling peoples across the vast Sahel region, they are cattle keepers, growing sorghum and

Mende singers accompany a performer on the shake-shake, a gourd rattle. Traditional singing in Sierre Leone is closely linked to dance, storytelling, and drama.

Most Mande-speaking men in the south work as farmers, growing rice, sorghum, millet, oil palms, and kola trees. The women fish in rivers with nets.

Life for Mande-speakers in the south is organized around secret societies, which guide and shape everyday life for men and women. Societies start by teaching children the rules of good behavior and all kinds of useful knowledge they will need in the adult world. They also hold ceremonies marking rites of passage, such as the change from a child to an adult or from being single to married. Senior members of these secret fellowships often act as leaders for the whole society.

The Kuranko people, from the remote mountain region in the northeast, speak a

Let's Talk Krio

The Krio language is a mixture of English, Portuguese, and various African languages. Here are some Krio words and phrases. You can see their similarities to English.

aw dee bohdhi? (AW dee-boe-dee)	*how are you feeling?*
moh-nin-o! (moe-NEEN-oe)	*good morning!*
wetin na yu nem? (weh-tih-nah-yoo-NEHM)	*what's your name?*
tap (TAHP)	*stop*
a wan wata? (ah-wahn-WAH-tah)	*please can I have some water?*
wi de go jisnoh (wee-dae-goe-jihz-noe)	*we're going now*
wetman (*from English*) (WEHT-mahn)	*European*
pumwe (*from Tembe*) (POOM-wae)	*European*
ow mus? (ow-MUSH)	*how much?*

millet where they can find reliable water supplies. They live and work together with the neighboring Loko and Kuranko.

In the past Krio people adopted certain European and African customs. However, their way of life has been badly disrupted by war, and their cultural influence has been declining throughout the twentieth century. Today many of Sierra Leone's professionals and intellectuals are Krio. Some carefully keep up British-style social conditions and wear formal British-style clothing.

Among the smaller groups in Sierra Leone, the Mandingo and Fulani traditionally work as traders and artisans; the Fulani are also cattle herders and day laborers. Both groups are Muslim. The Limba are farmers who live in north-central Sierra Leone.

Life in Sierra Leone Today

Because of the war, the whole country is a dangerous place to live. Gangs of rebels, bandits, diamond smugglers, and out-of-control government soldiers, all armed with guns, raid villages and towns, set up roadblocks, and attack, rob, and kill passers-by. During the war the RUF rebels captured or recruited children as young as ten and initiated them into the brutalities of war. Some of these brutalities included hacking off limbs from children and elderly men and women who failed to support them.

Until recent years, most people in Sierra Leone lived in the countryside and supported themselves by growing food and raising animals to feed their families. They grew crops such as rice and cassava (in the south) and millet and sorghum (in the north) for local consumption, together with coffee, cocoa, palm kernels, peanuts, and ginger, which they grew for cash.

However, when the fighting began in 1991, many farming people sought shelter in the capital and smaller towns. Most of these refugees survived by finding what work they could, by begging, or on food handouts from overseas aid organizations. After Freetown was attacked in 1998, thousands of people moved back to the countryside again in fear of their lives. There, many found that government

---

The Krio Factor

Between 1808 and 1864 at least seventy thousand western African slaves, rescued from slave ships, were settled in and around Freetown. They lived alongside former slaves who had returned to Africa from North America, Great Britain, and the Caribbean. Few of these returnees originally came from Sierra Leone. Many had been taught the Christian religion. Some were educated and could read and write. Others brought with them a heritage of languages and religious beliefs from their Wolof (WOE-lawf), Bambara (bahm-BAH-rah), and Yoruba (YOE-roo-bah) homelands. Some returnees married European sailors or merchants. Others married people from African cultures other than their own.

In this way a new Krio (or Creole) civilization developed, part African and part European. Krio people wore European-style clothes, went to European-style schools, and worshiped in Christian churches. They worked alongside Europeans as traders and missionaries, joined the British army and frontier police, and worked in the British administration.

Mende women crush fruit from palm trees to make thick, orange-red palm oil. Locally it's used for cooking, but it's also exported for use in soaps, detergents, and skin-care products.

soldiers or rebels had destroyed their homes. Today many families are homeless and hungry, living in makeshift camps and shelters, where they struggle to survive.

During the fighting the health-care system almost entirely collapsed. There is serious malnutrition, polluted drinking water, and a grave shortage of medical staff and supplies. Many people die because they cannot get treatment for the terrible injuries and mutilations they received in battles and raids. Even in peacetime, Sierra Leone's warm, moist climate is an ideal environment for dangerous diseases to breed.

Until the war, the government ran a good educational program, but many schools and colleges have been destroyed during the war, and many teachers have been killed.

Sierra Leone has rich resources of minerals, chiefly diamonds, bauxite, and titanium, plus fertile land and plenty of rainfall for growing export crops. Potentially profitable fishing grounds also lie off the coast. However, because of corruption and poor planning by past governments, well-managed businesses or mines are few, power supplies are erratic, and potholes cover the roads. There are, however, some small-scale factories making goods for home consumption, such as cloth, cigarettes, shoes, and beer. In the north and east, valuable timber is harvested from the rain forests.

The war has also seriously damaged the economy. All the important mines have been closed. Most diamonds are

Weeding young rice seedlings in flooded fields is very hard work. Farmers also risk the danger of catching diseases from bacteria and animals in the stagnant waters.

Cars and trucks jam the streets of Freetown. This picture was taken shortly before rebels attacked the city in 1999. Many houses and shops were looted and destroyed.

illegally smuggled out of the country. The profitable fishing and tourist industries have collapsed. After the United Nations imposed economic sanctions in 1997 to put pressure on the leaders of the army coup, the value of trade, industry, and commerce fell by 40 percent. Today there are shortages of foods and fuels, runaway inflation, and massive foreign debt.

Freetown: Gateway to Sierra Leone

Freetown, the capital of Sierra Leone, is built on an attractive site on steep slopes between the mountains and beautiful beaches. Its coastal location and sheltered deep-water harbor made it one of the world's most important ports for over one hundred years. It was used as a refueling station, where supplies of coal could be loaded on steamships before the ships would depart on long ocean voyages.

Freetown's architecture is mainly in Krio style: low-rise buildings with courtyards and balconies, covered in plaster and brightly painted or whitewashed. A few early-nineteenth-century wood-framed Krio houses still survive. There are also many crowded and crime-ridden slums. Since war broke out in the early 1990s, the city's housing and water supplies have been severely stretched by thousands of refugees fleeing the war in the countryside. Rampaging armies have also attacked and looted many residential areas. The city is especially dangerous at night.

Rice and Sauce

Rice is the staple food, along with plantains, mashed cassava, and cornmeal. All these are served with *plasas* (PLAH-zahs), a sauce

Members of a women's craft cooperative making gara *cloth, which is colored deep blue with indigo (made from plants) and tie-dyed in complicated patterns.*

Arts and Music

There is little artistic activity in Sierra Leone today, but over the centuries its peoples have created a variety of arts and crafts. Artisans in the north produce beautiful fabrics. The best known are "country cloth," handwoven cotton strips joined together, and *gara* (GAH-rah), brightly colored patterns using batik or tie-dye techniques. Temne women weave big round *shukublai* (SHKOOB-lie) baskets out of dyed raffia and grass.

Sierra Leone also has a long tradition of music, played on local instruments such as drums; *balanga* (buh-LAHN-gah), or xylophones; *khandi* (KAHN-dee), or thumb pianos; and shake-shake, or gourd rattles. *Mringa* (muh-REENG-gah), Krio music, uses Western instruments.

made from cassava leaves, palm oil, and fish or beef, or with okra sauce, peanut or palm-oil stew, or pepper soup. *Bench* (BEHCH)—beans with palm oil and fish—is another popular dish. There are chop bars (cheap, simple eating houses) in many places and also stalls selling take-out food, such as roasted sweet corn, fried plantains or yams, and doughnuts. For desserts or snacks, tropical fruits such as mangoes, oranges, limes, and tangerines are popular. Favorite drinks include local beer, palm wine, ginger beer (nonalcoholic), and coffee.

Masks and wood carvings for sale in a Freetown shop. Crafts like these are based on traditional designs and techniques.

SOMALIA

SOMALIA IN EASTERN AFRICA is a land of dry, hot desert.

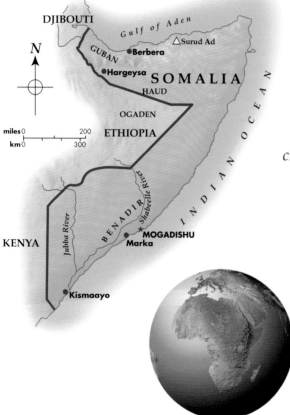

Somalia's coast on the Gulf of Aden is bordered by the Guban, a dry, scrub-covered plain. This rises to a chain of cliffs and mountains extending from the Ethiopian border to the far east. The highest point is Surud Ad, which rises 7,894 feet (2,406 meters) above sea level. Central Somalia is occupied by the Haud Plateau, but the south is a land of plains crossed by the Jubba and Shabeelle Rivers.

In the dry and dusty northwest, a Somali nomad attaches a frame on the back of a camel to carry the matting she uses to make her shelter.

CLIMATE

Northern Somalia is very hot and humid but with a low rainfall. The central plateau region is cooler. The highest rainfall is on the southern plains.

	Mogadishu	**Berbera**
Average January temperature:	79°F (26°C)	76°F (24°C)
Average July temperature:	78°F (26°C)	97°F (36°C)
Average annual precipitation:	17 in. (43 cm)	2 in. (5 cm)

On the Horn of Africa

Little is known of the ancient history of Somalia (soe-MAH-lee-uh). Rock paintings and carvings found in the north confirm that the region was occupied in Stone Age times. The hot, dusty landscape was the home of

FACTS AND FIGURES

Official name: *Jamhuriyadda Dimugradiga Somaliya (Somali Democratic Republic)*

Status: *Independent state*

Capital: *Mogadishu*

Major towns: *Hargeysa, Marka, Kismaayo, Berbera*

Area: *246,154 square miles (637,539 square kilometers)*

Population: *7,100,000*

Population density: *29 per square mile (11 per square kilometer)*

Peoples: *98 percent Somali; 2 percent other*

Official languages: *Somali and Arabic*

Currency: *Somali shilling*

National days: *Independence Day (June 26); Foundation of the Republic Day (July 1)*

Country's name: *Somalia means "land of milk," referring to the traditional diet of the nomadic herders.*

nomadic herders, ancestors of today's Somali and also of the Oromo peoples, who now mostly live in Ethiopia (see ETHIOPIA). From about thirteen hundred years ago, Persians and Muslim Arabs founded trading ports such as Mogadishu (moe-guh-DEE-shoo) around the coastline. Their wooden sailing ships, or dhows, traded far across the Indian Ocean and down the eastern African coast and islands.

Islam soon took root in Somalia, and mosques still stand that date back to the 1200s C.E. City-states ruled by sultans (Muslim kings) developed. One of the most powerful of these states was called

Zeila, located near what is now the Djibouti border. The sultans became increasingly powerful, expanding their territory to the south and west and by the 1300s were clashing with the ancient Christian empire of Ethiopia.

By the 1500s the Somali sultans faced a new enemy—the Portuguese, whose aim was to dominate Indian Ocean trade. Soon other Europeans were also sailing into these waters to challenge the Arabs, Indians, and Portuguese.

Inland regions of Somalia attracted few visitors. The landscape was harsh and dry, and the people were divided into warring clans (groups sharing descent from a common ancestor). By the early nineteenth century, Somali power was declining as its rulers fought each other in endless feuds. The Ethiopian Empire took over the Ogaden (oe-GAH-den) Desert region, the homeland of many Somali herders. The Sultanate of Oman annexed southern Somalia, too, as part of its growing eastern African coastal empire, which stretched southward to Zanzibar (see TANZANIA).

Europeans Divide the Land

By 1869 the Suez Canal had opened, giving European shipping a direct route to the Red Sea. The European powers now wished to control the southern approach to the Red Sea. Between 1884 and 1887 Great Britain created the Protectorate of British Somaliland in the north. In 1889 Italy purchased southern Somali territory from the Sultan of Oman to create another European protectorate in the south. Somali

Time line:	Arab settlers bring Islam; Mogadishu founded	Somali states expand, clash with Ethiopians	Somali power declines; Ethiopian Empire takes Ogaden Desert; Sultanate of Oman annexes southern Somalia	Protectorates of British Somaliland and Italian Somaliland created
	ca. 700 C.E.	1000s–1300s	1800s	1880s

resistance to both new colonial powers was fierce. Led by a religious leader named Mohammad Abdille Hassan, the resistance lasted from 1899 until his death in 1921.

In 1936 Italy conquered Ethiopia and united it with Italian Somaliland to create Italian East Africa. However, World War II (1939–1945) broke out three years later, and Great Britain and Italy became enemies. British troops occupied southern Somalia in 1941. The Somali had not abandoned the dream of regaining their freedom, and in 1943 they founded the first nationalist political party, the Somali Youth League. In 1950 the United Nations returned southern Somaliland to Italian rule.

Ten years later, the British and Italian territories were united and became an independent republic. The new country soon ran into conflict over its borders with Kenya and Ethiopia. In 1969 there was a coup, and Major General Muhammad Siad Barre seized power. Political parties were banned by the new Supreme Revolutionary Council. The 1970s saw severe droughts, which killed many thousands of people, and renewed fighting with Ethiopia over the Ogaden region. Somalia was defeated and had to endure long years of war between rival political factions.

In 1991 rebel fighters captured the capital, Mogadishu, and the Siad Barre government fled. All central rule collapsed, and the country broke up into regions dominated by heavily armed clan chiefs. Famine threatened 1.5 million Somali, and

Somali women walk through a badly damaged area of Mogadishu. The streets of the capital were devastated by fighting between rival clans and warlords during the 1990s.

local warlords seized international food aid intended for the starving.

In 1992 the United Nations sent in an international military force in an attempt to save the starving people and restore order. However, fighting between rival warlords continued, and the UN withdrew in 1995. A peace agreement was reached in 1997, but general chaos still prevailed. By 1999 Islamic leaders and local business interests were joining forces to put an end to the continuing lack of law, order, and stable government.

British and Italian territories united as independent republic	Coup by Muhammad Siad Barre; political parties banned	Unsuccessful war against Ethiopia over Ogaden	Civil war begins	Rebels capture Mogadishu	Peace agreement
1960	**1969**	**1977–1978**	**1982**	**1991**	**1997**

Agriculture and Industry

Only 1.6 percent of Somalia is suitable for growing crops, located mostly in the south, around the Jubba (JOO-bah) and Shabeelle (sha-BEH-lee) Rivers. Here, enough rain falls to grow sugarcane and bananas. Other crops include cotton, peanuts, sesame, and sorghum, a hardy grain crop. Three-quarters of all Somali are still herders, most of them nomadic, wandering the dry, scrubby landscape with their herds of camels, goats, sheep, and cattle.

Animal hides and livestock are an important export. As in ancient times, myrrh—the resin made from the sap of a spiny shrub—is included on the list of exports.

Industry employs only 8 percent of the workforce. Textiles are produced, locally caught fish are canned, and there is a sugar refinery. Oil and natural gas have been found, but these and other mineral resources have yet to be exploited.

Ways of Life

A majority of Somali live in poverty, and years of war and famine have brought many to the brink of disaster. Health care has been minimal during these troubles. Life expectancy is only forty-seven years for men and fifty-one years for women. Out of every 1,000 children, 176 die before they are five.

State education has been missed by many children, although they are supposed to receive eight years of schooling. Koranic schools, at which children learn the holy scriptures of Islam, have continued to thrive. Only 36 percent of adult men and 14 percent of adult women can read and write; these literacy rates reflect the view in Somali society that women do not need an education.

The Somali diet is often sparse. A typical meal is based around *anjeera* (ahn-JEE-rah), which is a thick, doughy bread; rice; and macaroni or spaghetti. These may be served with a sauce or stew, with liver, onions, or, on special occasions, with mutton or goat. Coastal waters provide lobster, crab, and tuna. Tropical fruits include bananas, mangoes, and papayas. Tea is the most popular drink.

The leaves of a bush called *qat* (KAHT) are chewed, not as a food but as a stimulant. The drug helps people stay awake. It is officially illegal in Somalia but has always been widely used.

Only a quarter of the population lives in towns such as Mogadishu, Hargeysa (hahr-GAE-suh), Berbera (BUHR-buh-ruh), and

Somali women nomads gather in their shelter. A cooking pot simmers on the hearth. One woman is pounding corn into cornmeal; the other is sorting cowpeas (black-eyed peas).

461

Let's Talk Somali

The Somali language has various dialects, but the standard version of the language is based on the northern form. Its spellings and forms were only standardized in 1972.

iska warran   *hello*
   (ISH-kah wah-RAHN)

fadlan   *please*
   (FAHD-lahn)

mahadsanid   *thank you*
   (mahd-sah-NEED)

nabad galyo   *good-bye*
   (nuh-BAHD GAHL-yoe)

haa   *yes*
   (HAH)

maya   *no*
   (MAE-yah)

Kismaayo (kees-MAH-yoe). The life of the nomadic herders who live in the interior is dominated by seasonal variations in water supply. They mostly travel in groups of about 150 people, made up of several extended family groups, including grandparents, parents, aunts, uncles, and children. Men are allowed to have up to four wives. It is the job of the men to herd the camels and the job of women and children to herd goats, sheep, and cattle. It is usually the women who set up camp. Shelters are dome-shaped, with a framework of branches covered with mats of straw.

Somalia is unusual in Africa in that almost all of the population belongs to the same ethnic group and to the same religion, Islam. The Somali are divided into about

A nomadic Somali family sits together by their campfire as the mother uses burning twigs to sterilize the inside of a milking vessel before scouring it clean.

one hundred clans. Loyalty to the clan counts above everything, and disputes among clans often erupt into long-standing feuds or bitter quarrels.

Somali live in many other countries as well as Somalia. Their homeland extends into neighboring Ethiopia, Kenya, and Djibouti (see ETHIOPIA, KENYA, and

This woman symbolizes the Somali ideal of beauty. She wears a colorful woven headband; long, beaded earrings and necklace, and markings painted on her cheeks and forehead.

A Tradition — Or Just a Crime?

More than 95 percent of young girls in Somalia undergo a genital cutting procedure in order to "become a woman." Variations of this practice are common in Ethiopia, Eritrea, Djibouti, Egypt, Sudan, Kenya, and many parts of central and western Africa. It is based on widely held African beliefs about fertility, and it is not confined to any specific religion.

The ritual is known as female genital cutting. Both men and women in these cultures believe that it aids health and beauty and ensures that women stay faithful to their husbands. It may lead to extreme pain and blood loss, infections, and a loss of sexual feeling. Plus, there is a very high risk of dangerous medical problems later in life.

The practice of genital cutting has been outlawed in several African countries and is condemned by many African women now living in Europe and North America. Among these campaigners is Waris Derie, a Somali woman now working as a fashion model in New York. As a young girl in the Somali desert, she experienced the terrifying pain of genital cutting. "It was nothing but torture," she says today.

DJIBOUTI). Other Somali have immigrated to Yemen, Saudi Arabia, the United Arab Emirates, and Europe.

Somali women wear long wraps of brightly colored cotton, tied at the right shoulder, and head scarves. Ornate jewelry is made from gold and silver. Men wear the *futa* (FOO-tah), which is a white robe, and a small, round, white hat.

The Somali have a great tradition of poetry, based on the spoken word rather than written literature. Poets create long complex poems on subjects such as history and politics and recite them on public occasions. Marriage feasts, religious festivals, and other important events are also marked by dancing.

Glossary

AIDS: *a*cquired *i*mmuno*d*eficiency *s*yndrome, a normally fatal disease often passed on by sexual intercourse. It is caused by the virus HIV (*h*uman *i*mmunodeficiency *v*irus), which attacks the body's ability to resist disease and infection.

annex: to take over adjoining territory, often without consultation.

assimilate: to mix one minority group of people within a predominant group of people.

batik: brightly-patterned cloth, produced by a complicated dyeing process. A pattern is painted on cloth with wax; then the cloth is dyed, and finally the wax is melted off, leaving the pattern in reverse.

cassava: a plant with fleshy tuber roots, used as a food.

cease-fire: a military order to stop fighting.

CFA franc: franc de la Communauté Financière Africaine (franc of the African Financial Community). This is a unit of currency shared by various African countries that were formerly French colonies.

chutney: a sauce or relish made of both sweet and sour ingredients, such as fruit, vegetables, spices, and other seasoning. Chutneys are commonly served with Indian meals.

consumption: the purchase and use of goods and produce.

coup: a change of government brought about by force.

economic sanctions: measures taken to prevent or limit trade with a particular country. The aim is to force that country to change its political system or its policies.

European Union: an alliance of European nations committed to economic union and closer political integration. It developed out of the European Economic Community (founded in 1957).

exodus: the departure or emigration of a large number of people.

garrison: a place where soldiers are housed.

indentured: working to fulfill a long-term contract of employment. In the colonial period, indentured laborers often surrendered many basic employment rights.

indigenous: relating to a people who were born within a country or a region as opposed to being immigrants or settlers. Also *aboriginal* or *native*.

Koranic schools: classrooms attached to mosques (buildings where Muslim people pray). Boys go there to learn how to read Arabic and to study the faith of Islam.

left-wing: pursuing radical, progressive, or socialist politics.

mercenaries: hired soldiers, people who fight for money.

militia: a group of ordinary citizens organized for military service; they are not a part of the regular army of a country and are used only in emergencies.

millet: a hardy cereal crop grown for food, drink, and fodder.

nationalism: a loyalty or devotion to a country; the promotion of policies designed to benefit and support a particular nation.

nationalize: to make something the property of the nation or state.

overlord: a senior or high-ranking official

plantains: fruit similar to bananas. They are a staple food in many tropical countries.

protectorate: a territory that is given the protection of a more powerful state. In the colonial period in Africa the "protection" was often just a ploy by European countries to achieve political control of the territory.

republic: a country in which power rests with the people and their elected representatives. A president usually heads a republic.

right-wing: favoring conservative and antireformist politics.

savanna: a grassland dotted with trees and drought-resistant undergrowth.

socialism: a political theory in which the community as a whole controls land, property, industry, and money, and organizes them for the good of all the people.

socialist: someone who believes in the theory of socialism.

sorghum: a grain crop commonly grown in hot countries.

subsidy: money provided by a government to keep the price of goods low.

subsistence farming: growing crops for one's own use rather than selling them.

tenacious: adhering or clinging to in a determined or persevering way.

terra-cotta: unglazed, brown-red pottery.

vote rigging: falsifying the results of an election, for example, by having people vote more than once for a candidate.

Further Reading

Internet Sites
Look under Countries A to Z in the Atlapedia Online Web Site at
　　　http://www.atlapedia.com/online/countries
Look under country listing in the CIA World Factbook Web Site at
　　　http://www.odci.gov/cia/publications/factbook
Look under country listing in the Library of Congress Country Studies Web Site at
　　　http://lcweb2.loc.gov/frd/cs/cshome.html

Réunion
See web sites mentioned above

Rwanda
Bodnarchuk, Kari. *Rwanda: A Country Torn Apart.* Minneapolis, MN: Lerner Publishing Group, 1997.
Freeman, Charles. *Crisis in Rwanda.* Orlando, FL: Raintree Steck-Vaughn, 1998.
Isaac, John, and Keith Elliot Greenberg. *Rwanda: Fierce Clashes in Central Africa.* Woodbridge, CT: Blackbirch Press, 1996.
Pomeray, J. K., and Sandra Stotsky. *Rwanda.* Broomall, PA: Chelsea House, 2000.
Twagilmana, Aimable, and Vincent Emenike Childwende. *Hutu and Tutsi.* New York: Rosen Group, 1997.
Twagilmana, Aimable. *Teenage Refugees from Rwanda Speak Out.* New York: Rosen Group, 1997.

Saint Helena
See web sites mentioned above

São Tomé and Príncipe
Aniakor, Chike C. *Fang.* New York: Rosen Group, 1996.

Senegal
Beaton, Margaret. *Senegal.* Danbury, CT: Children's Press, 1997.
Berg, Elizabeth L. *Senegal.* Tarrytown, NY: Marshall Cavendish, 1999.
Ndukwe, Pat I. *Fulani.* New York: Rosen Group, 1995.
Sallah, Tijan M. *Wolof.* New York: Rosen Group, 1996.

Seychelles
See web sites mentioned above

Sierra Leone
See web sites mentioned above

Somalia
Fox, Mary Virginia. *Somalia.* Danbury, CT: Children's Press, 1996.
Hassig, Susan. *Somalia.* Tarrytown, NY: Benchmark Books, 1997.
Hussein, Ikram. *Teenage Refugees from Somalia Speak Out.* New York: Rosen Group, 1997.
Matthews, Jo. *I Remember Somalia.* Orlando, FL: Raintree Steck-Vaughn, 1994.
Nnoromele, Salome C. *Somalia.* San Diego, CA: Lucent Books, 2000.

Index

Page numbers in *italic* indicate illustrations.

Page numbers in *italic* indicate illustrations.